Effective Teachers

A reflective resource for enhancing practice

VITAL - Video & Internet Teaching Across Lands

A video support book

Tony Swainston

Sponsored by:

Published by Network Educational Press Ltd.
PO Box 635
Stafford
ST16 1BF

First Published 2002
© Tony Swainston 2002

ISBN 1 85539 125 2

Quotations from *A Model of Teacher Effectiveness: Report by Hay McBer to the
Department for Education and Employment - June 2000* (DfEE Publications, © Crown
Copyright 2000), are reproduced by permission of the Controller of
Her Majesty's Stationery Office.

Series Editor: Prof Tim Brighouse
Project Manager: Anne Oppenheimer
Design & layout: Neil Hawkins, Network Educational Press Ltd.
Illustrations by Tony Swainston
Cover illustration by Annabel Spenceley

Printed in Great Britain by
MPG Books Ltd., Bodmin, Cornwall

About the author

Tony Swainston has taught for eighteen years in three comprehensive schools. His work has included being a pastoral head for eleven years, and, therefore, experiencing at first hand the great impact effective teachers can have on the development and behaviour of pupils. He is a member of the Leadership Group in his school with responsibilities which include sharing good practice with other schools through Beacon Status and overseeing the programme for gifted and talented pupils in the school.

Tony's wife is a teacher and they have three children.

Tony is a member of the Teacher Training Agency 'National Teacher Research Panel'.

Foreword

A teacher's task is much more ambitious than it used to be and demands a focus on the subtleties of teaching and learning and on the emerging knowledge of school improvement.

This is what this series is about.

Teaching can be a very lonely activity. The time-honoured practice of a single teacher working alone in the classroom is still the norm; yet to operate alone is, in the end, to become isolated and impoverished. This series addresses two issues – the need to focus on practical and useful ideas connected with teaching and learning and the wish thereby to provide some sort of an antidote to the loneliness of the long-distance teacher who is daily berated by an anxious society.

Teachers flourish best when, in key stage teams or departments (or more rarely whole schools), their talk is predominantly about teaching and learning and where, unconnected with appraisal, they are privileged to observe each other teach; to plan and review their work together; and to practise the habit of learning from each other new teaching techniques. But how does this state of affairs arise? Is it to do with the way staffrooms are physically organized so that the walls bear testimony to interesting articles and in the corner there is a dedicated computer tuned to 'conferences' about SEN, school improvement, the teaching of English etc., and whether, in consequence, the teacher leaning over the shoulder of the enthusiastic IT colleague sees the promise of interesting practice elsewhere? Has the primary school cracked it when it organizes successive staff meetings in different classrooms and invites the 'host' teacher to start the meeting with a 15 minute exposition of their classroom organization and management? Or is it the same staff sharing, on a rota basis, a slot on successive staff meeting agenda when each in turn reviews a new book they have used with their class? And what of the whole school which now uses 'active' and 'passive' concerts of carefully chosen music as part of their accelerated learning techniques?

It is of course well understood that even excellent teachers feel threatened when first they are observed. Hence the epidemic of trauma associated with OFSTED. The constant observation of the teacher in training seems like that of the learner driver. Once you have passed your test and can drive unaccompanied, you do. You often make lots of mistakes and sometimes get into bad habits. Woe betide, however, the back seat driver who tells you so. In the same way, the new teacher quickly loses the habit of observing others and being observed. So how do we get a confident, mutual observation debate going? One school I know found a simple and therefore brilliant solution. The Head of the History Department asked that a young colleague plan lessons for her – the Head of Department – to teach. This lesson she then taught, and was observed by the young colleague. There was subsequent discussion, in which the young teacher asked,

> *"Why did you divert the question and answer session I had planned?"*

and was answered by,

> *"Because I could see that I needed to arrest the attention of the group by the window with some 'hands-on' role play, etc."*

This lasted an hour and led to a once-a-term repeat discussion which, in the end, was adopted by the whole school. The whole school subsequently changed the pattern of its meetings to consolidate extended debate about teaching and learning. The two teachers claimed that, because one planned and the other taught, both were implicated but neither alone was responsible or felt 'got at'.

So there are practices which are both practical and more likely to make teaching a rewarding and successful activity. They can, as it were, increase the likelihood of a teacher surprising the pupils into understanding or doing something they did not think they could do rather than simply entertaining them or worse still occupying them. There are ways of helping teachers judge the best method of getting pupil expectation just ahead of self-esteem.

This series focuses on straightforward interventions which individual schools and teachers use to make life more rewarding for themselves and those they teach. Teachers deserve nothing less, for they are the architects of tomorrow's society, and society's ambition for what they achieve increases as each year passes.

Professor Tim Brighouse

Contents

Acknowledgements

I am eternally grateful to all those teachers who have allowed me to film in their classrooms, and for all the help and guidance offered to me by colleagues who have read through and commented on my ideas. Four years ago I started discussions concerning VITAL with Gervase Phinn, then a Senior Adviser in North Yorkshire and now a successful author. I am grateful for the time and encouragement Gervase gave me at this initial stage. I owe particular thanks to John Freeman, Senior Adviser in Leeds, for allowing me over the past four years to talk through my ideas, which has resulted in the video material and manual which comprises VITAL. Chris Edwards and Education Leeds have also given support and encouragement throughout the making of the VITAL videos and the writing of this book.

My thanks also go out to my close friend Pascal Gosteau from the Chamber of Commerce in France for again helping to bring about the idea of VITAL over a glass of St Emilion whilst on holiday in the Alps. I have been extremely fortunate to work for Anne Clarke, a headteacher whose open-minded approach to my ideas has allowed this project to develop.

Most importantly, thank you to my wife, who has put up with my ramblings over a long period of time whilst teaching full-time herself and managing to bring up three beautiful children. (My oldest daughter, Victoria, has also kindly helped me to type out this manual.)

I owe a great deal to all five of the teachers featured in VITAL who kindly volunteered to be filmed. I also thank the other teachers who were filmed during the course of the project but were not included in the final video (but could easily have been).

Angliacampus, BT and Transco have all provided sponsorship to allow this project to happen. Leeds Metropolitan University filmed the teachers in the classrooms in England. I am indebted to Elspeth Jones from Leeds Metropolitan University for her kind encouragement and support of the project, and to Mike Hooper, Andy Riley, Bob Bajorek and Paul Wilmott for their professional approach throughout all the filming.

And last but not least, thank you to my partners in France and Spain, Marylène Gosteau and Maria Jesus Vives, for all the work they have done in filming teachers in Valenciennes and Barcelona. Their work will be included in the next part of the VITAL project, which will be available next year.

Tony Swainston
December 2001

The VITAL Project – Introduction

'On the threshold of a dream'

All teachers dream of a classroom where they work in harmony with pupils who behave well and are hungry to learn. I believe this is possible if, as teachers, we are all continually learning from the tremendous abilities possessed by effective teachers around us.

This manual and the videos which accompany it are intended to assist teachers in their movement towards, and ultimately through, the 'threshold of their dream'.

We can all learn to improve and to be more effective as teachers, no matter how proficient and skilled we are already. This is the core belief that runs through VITAL. We are in a profession where we encourage pupils to continually want to improve, and the best way we can achieve this is to demonstrate that we ourselves believe in continuous development and growth in our work as teachers – that we ourselves embrace the concept of lifelong learning. The Hay McBer Report makes this clear as follows:

> The commitment of teachers to their own continuing professional development reminds them of what it is like to be a learner, and helps them develop their own skills and characteristics. This helps them to empathise with pupils, and models the importance of continuous lifelong learning.

Tony Attwood has expressed how the result of a teaching approach which involves a desire for continuous improvement can in the end provide more efficiency and less stress:

> *The issue is rather like learning to swim. It is quite possible to learn to swim, and avoid drowning, without being much good at swimming. Someone who has studied swimming technique, however, might be able to show you how to swim in a much more efficient way – more output for less input. More result for less stress. Even an expert swimmer can improve – can squeeze that extra one hundredth of a second out of a swimming length. The same is true in teaching.*
>
> *Tony Attwood*

The name VITAL grew out of an idea I had to video teachers in different countries in order to compare different teaching styles. Through video evidence and an internet-website I wished to illustrate the similarities of effective teaching in different countries, together with the unique characteristics which may develop from a cultural base. This is why I named the project VITAL. VITAL is an acronym for 'Video and Internet Teaching Across Lands'. I have now gathered video evidence of teachers from three major

European cities – Leeds, Barcelona and Valenciennes. Stage 1 of the VITAL project is called *Effective Teachers* and analyses the style of the five English teachers who were filmed.

Analysis of the teachers draws heavily on the Hay McBer Report, which was released in June 2000. At the moment I believe the Hay McBer Report is a very valuable but underused piece of research. Part of the reason why it has not been extensively used in a lot of schools is down to the lack of time that teachers feel they have for studying reports such as this one. My hope is that the VITAL project will bring the Hay McBer Report to life and demonstrate its real value. VITAL Stage 2 will be released in 2002 and will compare the teaching styles of the teachers from the three different countries.

The sections from the lessons you see on the videos are not set-up situations. Sometimes the classes were not told until immediately before entering the classroom that they were going to be filmed. I wanted to capture as much as possible real-life classroom experiences. It is of course true to say that as soon as you bring another individual (an OFSTED inspector for example!!) into the classroom the children will change and behave differently (and the teacher certainly, in the case of the OFSTED inspector!!). The aim of the video, however, is to provide you with examples of real teachers in real lessons who are effective practitioners in the art of teaching and interacting with their classes.

This project started in my mind some four years ago and developed from my experience over a number of years as a Head of Year. I felt frustrated that I was often dealing with the same problems created by the same pupils in the same classrooms with the same teachers. These pupils were at times not presenting problems to other teachers, and although I often knew instinctively why this was I never found it easy to know how to suggest effective strategies to my colleagues and friends without it appearing to be patronizing. At the same time, however, I felt it was unfair to leave teachers to struggle with what they saw as difficult pupils. It has to be said that it was not fair at times on the pupil concerned either. I decided then that I would like to study what common characteristics could be uncovered for effective classroom teachers. The best way I thought this could then be shared by others was through making a video of teachers who demonstrated effective classroom techniques.

The pupils in VITAL may seem to be an unrepresentative sample of consistently 'well-behaved' individuals. I can assure you that these are normal pupils and that in different situations if they are bored and don't have the feeling that they are making progress, they appear differently. If you think yourself of different situations where you have been in lectures (first of all where you have been motivated by the content or presentation, and secondly, where the content and presentation has bored you) you will understand how pupils, like yourself, may appear different in different situations.

No one could claim that the teachers in VITAL can present all the possible ways of dealing with classes. Every teacher is different and indeed this, to me, is what makes teaching, and looking at methods of teaching, so exciting. What I hope you will be able to see, however, are a variety of methods of teaching which are successful, and which other teachers can learn something from.

The five English teachers in VITAL are from four schools in Leeds. As I have said, no one is saying that these teachers cover all the ways in which a teacher can teach effectively. What they do demonstrate, however, is a range of effective strategies that we can all learn something from. Mike Hughes, in his excellent book called *Closing the Learning Gap* said:

> *All schools have excellent teachers. More specifically, all schools have teachers who are wonderful exponents of particular aspects of classroom practice, whose expertise should and could be shared with others.*
>
> Mike Hughes

This is what VITAL aims to do. That is, it provides a convenient vehicle for all teachers to look at and share the expertise of others. Sometimes it is not easy to find the time within the constraints of a normal teaching week to be able to observe colleagues and draw valuable conclusions in a considered way. One of the benefits of VITAL is that it can be used:

- as a mechanism for discussion during school INSET concerning classroom management

- by individual teachers at home who may wish to review their own approach to teaching as all good professionals should do

- by ITT students who may wish to supplement their own classroom observation with examples of effective teachers in other schools

- by training colleges who wish to give their classroom students examples of effective teachers and use this as a means of discussion

- by teachers who are reflecting on their classroom teaching practice as the approach to their Threshold application

- by teachers who are reflecting on their classroom teaching practice as they move through the stages of 'performance management'.

More than anything else, my work on the VITAL project has reinforced the already high regard I had for teachers. Like so many teachers who know that they and their colleagues work very hard, I find it extremely annoying when so much of the press we receive is negative and downbeat.

In addition, rewarding as teaching may be – and I believe it is extremely rewarding – being a teacher is nevertheless an extremely exhausting occupation. If nothing else, this alone is surely a good reason for attempting to spread the good practice which exists in schools so that individuals are not working in a vacuum but rather benefiting from the skills, expertise and vast experience of other teachers. This has traditionally been the practice to some extent within subject areas, but not so common within the broader field of looking at general good teaching and learning skills, though this is now changing.

The culture of sharing practice within schools may be now changing for the better, with teaching and learning starting, at last, to take its rightful position as the most important element in the development plan of many schools. I still believe, however, that we have a long way to go in breaking down the barriers of sugar paper that symbolically cover the glass on some classroom doors.

I am writing this present section at the end of a week which has seen the resignation of Chris Woodhead as Chief Inspector of OFSTED. I have felt the stress and tension which most teachers feel when the OFSTED inspectors arrive in your school. My predominant regret about OFSTED, however, is that with all the immense experience of good practice observed by inspectors in different schools there is not a better mechanism built into the system to allow schools to benefit from it. Phil Willis (the Liberal Democrat Shadow Secretary of State for Education and Employment) recently expressed this in a speech to members of his constituency in Harrogate. He said that he was dismayed that OFSTED was always seen as a overly judgmental organization in which the OFSTED inspectors' privilege of witnessing good practice in schools seemed to vanish, and not resurface for the benefit of the teaching profession.

Classroom management and classroom effectiveness is not something that can ever become a precise science. To believe that a formula can be arrived at which will allow teachers to find success in every conceivable situation is, to say the least, very naïve. I firmly believe, however, that we can all learn to be more effective practitioners in the classroom. Unfortunately this is not, in my experience, a view shared by all teachers. It seems to me that there is a clear dichotomy in the views of teachers, between those who believe that a teacher is either born with the innate skills required to be an effective teacher, or, alternatively, someone who will always struggle; and those who believe, as I do, that the greater part of classroom effectiveness can be learned.

It is perhaps true that individual character plays a significant part in the success of a teacher. The charismatic aspect of the teacher's role in the classroom cannot be denied. At the same time, however, I believe that many of the skills that make a teacher effective can be actively learned. I say 'actively learned' because the alternative is to hope that the skills are somehow stumbled upon by accident or acquired through experience. Some of this undoubtedly happens, but surely, as professionals, it is more advisable that we should not leave it to chance but rather seek to uncover the elements which go to make up an effective classroom practitioner. Knowledge born of experience as distinct from conceptual knowledge is important, but the barriers between practical and theoretical approaches to teaching should be torn down so that all teachers can benefit from the work of all

"Can someone out there ......
Somewhere .... help me?"

contributors to the art of teaching. In addition I would argue that some of what we refer to as the 'natural charisma' of an individual can also be learned by others. Anthony Robbins in his bestselling book *Unlimited Power* makes the argument for developing excellence through modelling very strongly. If we cling on to the view that we are what we are and there is no way to change this, then progress cannot be made. A central theme in VITAL is that by modelling ourselves on effective people we can ourselves become more effective. This is as true in teaching as it is in any other walk of life.

In a report published by the University of London's Institute of Education, Chris Watkins says that 'the classroom is the most complex and least understood situation on the face of the planet'.

This may be stretching it a bit – but not a lot, in my opinion. Again, Chris Watkins says: 'For 60 years studies have shown that the teacher's style of running a group has a major effect on young people's behaviour.' Teachers do make a difference to the

Effective Teachers

education of pupils. It is therefore important that all teachers should strive to be better at the fundamental basis of their work as effective classroom practitioners.

Running an efficient and happy classroom environment is a highly complex skill to master, with studies showing that teachers engage in 1,000 interactions a day – similar to an air traffic controller. I am convinced that by looking at techniques which are initially unfamiliar to us we may, once we adopt these techniques, eventually claim that they are 'common sense'. As a result, when we have studied classroom effectiveness we may feel that the good practice we encounter we already really knew about in the first place, and that it is indeed just common sense.

What we call common sense only feels natural when it is part of what you do on a regular basis. This is what Stephen R. Covey refers to as a 'habit'. Habits are things that can be good or bad for us. They can be modified or changed, but this is not necessarily easy and may involve a lot of effort to ensure that the habits we wish to maintain are constantly refreshed, and those we wish to get rid of are resisted. Covey says:

> As Horace Mann, the great educator, once said, 'Habits are like a cable. We weave a strand of it every day and soon it cannot be broken'. I personally do not agree with the last part of this expression. I know they can be broken. Habits can be learned and unlearned. But I also know it isn't a quick fix. It involves a process and tremendous commitment.
>
> *Stephen R. Covey*

The best way for something to become a habit is for us to see it in action and then try it out for ourselves. It is important for us to share the wealth of our experience because, as Plautus said:

> No man is wise enough by himself.
>
> *Plautus*

The aim of VITAL is to provide material which can be used for observation before it is tried out. Learning is a process of exploration. When an explorer journeys to a new and initially strange land, it takes a while before she can feel comfortable, settle down, and become familiar with the terrain. After a certain time, however, the new and strange land becomes part of her everyday experience, and in some ways it will feel to the explorer that she has always known this place. So it is with teachers who look at new ways of doing something. To begin with it will seem strange, but after a while it will seem quite natural – it will feel as if it was something you have always done. Education often takes us on a journey where we seem to arrive back where we started – and yet our understanding has improved a great deal. T. S. Eliot expressed this process of looking at ideas and the journey this takes us on, in the following way:

> We must not cease from exploration. And the end of all our exploring will be to arrive where we began and to know the place for the first time.
>
> *T. S. Eliot*

May I wish you well on your journey as a teacher who is always seeking to be more effective. I hope that the VITAL project proves to be of help to you in some small or more significant way.

Tony Swainston

Ways of using VITAL Stage 1

VITAL Stage 1 draws heavily on the findings of *A Model of Teacher Effectiveness. Report by Hay McBer to the Department for Education and Employment – June 2000*. The effectiveness of each of the five teachers on the video is therefore related to the written comments in the Hay McBer Report. A summary of the categories within the Report is given in Section 4 of VITAL Stage 1.

In Section 5 I will attempt to indicate some of the attributes (I have termed these 'key elements') that I think make each of the UK teachers effective as classroom practitioners. You may well disagree with me – this is not a bad thing. The very act of analysing the teachers is the most important thing you can do with VITAL. Indeed, you may well believe that attributes I have not included are the most important aspects of individual teachers' performance. In addition to my view of the key elements that make each teacher effective I have made reference to the Hay McBer Report and in particular 'teaching skills' and 'professional characteristics'. (I have illustrated the effectiveness of each teacher through one teaching skill and three professional characteristics.)

The written analysis here and the commentary on the edited video are there to serve and help you. There are different ways in which you may wish to use the information in VITAL:

1. You may wish to look at the near unedited, approximately 30-minute sections on each of the five teachers and draw your own conclusions first. You may then like to compare your analysis with the things I have highlighted about each teacher.

2. Alternatively, you may wish to look at the edited 20-minute video first, then read my comments on of the teachers before finally watching the 30-minute sections and adding your own views on what makes each teacher effective.

VITAL can be used by teachers with the following in mind:

- teachers in their Initial Teacher Training year. In this case it can by used by schools with ITT students, universities training teachers, teacher training colleges and individual ITT students

- teachers wishing to apply to go through the Threshold and looking for ways of demonstrating and improving upon their effectiveness

- teachers following the Performance Management route to enhance their career development

- (most importantly) all teachers who believe they can improve their own personal effectiveness as classroom teachers by observing others.

We must all, as teachers, be prepared to continually improve and adopt new methods of teaching and learning. The Hay McBer Report makes this clear:

> Effective teachers in the future will need to deal with a climate of continual change.

Schools may wish to use VITAL during INSET days, or individual teachers can view and study VITAL in the comfort of their own homes.

My experience of working on the VITAL project has convinced me that effective teachers are found throughout the whole range of the teaching profession. Again, the Hay McBer Report comes to this conclusion as well:

> We found that biometric data (i.e. information about teachers' age and teaching experience, additional responsibilities, qualifications, career history and so on) did not allow us to predict their effectiveness as a teacher. Effective and outstanding teachers came from diverse backgrounds… Effective and outstanding teachers teach in all kinds of schools and school contexts.

Effective Teachers

The ART and the ACT of being a teacher

Central to VITAL is the belief that all teachers should view their work in the classroom as an act that can be continuously improved upon. After a while the act will be fully integrated into the personality of the teacher – it will become a habit which feels totally natural. This chapter will look at the ways in which the art and act of teaching can be approached as a lifelong learning process in which the skills we employ can be continuously refined. In *Bridging the Learning Gap* Mike Hughes expresses the ongoing process of learning as a teacher as follows: 'It is a journey that will never end, because, no matter how effective a teacher, department or school, they can always improve.'

We can all learn and improve

The teachers on these videos know that they have set themselves up potentially to be shot down by other teachers watching the video. The cry of 'I don't think he/she is that good' is something they are all aware may happen. None of the teachers on the video, however, claims to have learned all there is to know about classroom techniques. The variety of styles they employ is testimony to the fact that there is a range of approaches which teachers can employ to achieve success. My discussions with them have revealed to me how they all rather think of themselves as students continuously learning and developing. What I can tell you, however, is that all of them are effective classroom teachers who are achieving very good results with their pupils.

The easiest thing we can do is to find fault with things – and given half a chance we are all experts at this. I set out with the aim of showing only positive aspects of teaching, and indeed this is what I believe VITAL shows. I have no doubt that if you wished to it would not be difficult to find fault with the teachers in VITAL. I would ask you to hold back from this, however, because I don't think it will achieve a great deal. It is far better to look for the positive in what they do and learn from this.
Henry Ford said:

> *Don't find fault, find a remedy.*
>
> *Henry Ford*

In the context of teaching and VITAL I want this to mean that the teachers on the videos should be used to find positive aspects of teaching and that these should be used for our own good – to find our own remedies.

The idea of learning by modelling our teaching performance on that of effective teachers is central to the VITAL project. By modelling other teachers we can learn in weeks what it would otherwise take us years (if ever) to learn. In a sense we all model ourselves on others all the time without being aware of it. We should, however, make modelling of others a more systematic process. What you yourself perceive to be the value or otherwise of strategies employed by the teachers in VITAL depends upon your own ways of viewing these teachers, and things in general. There is no definitive description of the teachers, or definitive truth about what they do, which will suit everyone. Einstein realized the limitations of trying to define an ultimate truth about anything:

> *Whoever undertakes to set himself up as a judge in the field of truth and knowledge is shipwrecked by the laughter of the gods.*
>
> *Albert Einstein*

Don't be trapped by limiting beliefs

It is very easy to be drawn into a belief system that says that you cannot improve, pupils are difficult, everything is stacked against you and you are the innocent victim. An alternative is to look for the possibilities which exist, and strive for improvement and success. I believe that this is what all effective teachers do. In my discussions with the teachers in the VITAL video it is clear that they all share an air of optimism and a desire to continuously improve. It is not a bad idea to spend a moment now thinking of five key beliefs about teaching and pupils that may at times have limited your progress, and then to think of another five statements about your personal beliefs which can serve to improve your performance and enjoyment of teaching. I believe it is important for you to derive your own examples here. I have included one limiting belief and one positive belief simply as examples. If these are relevant to you then please keep them; if not, then please ignore them.

Limiting beliefs	Positive beliefs
1. I always have trouble with 9H.	1. I enjoy praising pupils and will do it even more in the future.
2.	2.
3.	3.
4.	4.
5.	5.

What it is important to realize is that your limiting beliefs do not have to remain part of you. You may have believed these things at one time and you may believe them now, but you do not have to continue to see things this way.

The skills of the actor

Some people may believe that acting skills play no part in the effectiveness of a teacher. There is perhaps an understandable concern that if a teacher is acting, then she is not being sincere. Sincerity in a teacher is absolutely crucial – pupils will realize when a teacher is not behaving in a sincere manner. Standing in front of a class of 20 to 30 individuals, who may not be the most receptive audience you could wish for, is not, however, a natural or everyday occurrence for most people. It is therefore essential that a teacher should be able to perform in an effective manner, such that all of the signals she is giving out indicate an individual who is in control. She must come over as a confident and technically able performer.

One of the most interesting and unexpected aspects of the work I carried out with VITAL was the repeated comment by teachers on how acting skills should be incorporated into teacher training. This occurred on so many occasions that I decided to contact John Mee from the West Yorkshire Playhouse in Leeds for his comments. Following discussions with John and the teachers filmed for VITAL it is my firm opinion that acting skills should be directly taught to all teachers so that they can be more effective in the classroom. The use of the voice, body language and positioning for maximum effect in the classroom are all things we would like to believe we could do effectively. Many teachers will do these things very effectively, but generally because they have stumbled on these skills or, less likely, because they happen to have been involved in drama training at some stage. It seems to me illogical that such powerful skills should not be taught to all teachers.

Aristotle said:

> *We are what we repeatedly do. Excellence, then, is not an act, but a habit.*
>
> *Aristotle*

By learning acting skills, and also by copying the skills of effective classroom teachers, which we can do by watching the teachers in the VITAL videos, we can all improve our performance. Once we have then practised these skills on a number of occasions, they will become part of us. They become a habit and part of our character. The belief that teachers can improve by observing and modelling themselves on others is a critical element in the final outcome. In the end, as Anthony Robbins quotes, and as the old saying expresses it:

> *Whether you believe you can do something or you believe you can't, you are right.*
>
> *Anthony Robbins*

The confidence and belief system that can develop in a teacher when certain skills are learned was emphasized in the Hay McBer Report, which said that:

> Effective teachers believe in themselves... Effective teachers see themselves as, and act as, 'leading professionals'.

It is very important that we all act in certain ways that make our overall performance as effective as possible. Constantly looking at what we do and how we might be able to improve our performance will, at the very least, enable us to meet the new challenges which we will inevitably face as society changes. At the same time I believe it will allow us to constantly look afresh at our classroom interactions, and as a result bring us greater enjoyment, fulfilment and success.

In *The Art of Happiness* Howard Cutler says:

> '... there is a reciprocal relationship between a supple mind and the ability to shift perspective: a supple, flexible mind helps us address our problems from a variety of perspectives'.

Perhaps one of the key things we as teachers need to have is a supple, flexible mind in order that we are always open and receptive to ideas which can affect our lives as teachers. No matter how good an individual teacher may be, there is no doubt that in some aspect they could improve. An effective way to improve is to copy the excellence of others. VITAL is one way of allowing us to do this.

Tony Attwood has recently referred to the benefits of adopting a positive body language, both in terms of the improved effectiveness that this brings in the classroom, and as a spin-off directly related to it, a reduction in stress for the teacher: 'Our view is that adopting positive body language is such an obvious benefit to everyone in education that it is surprising that more people do not pay attention to it. Indeed it is more than likely that a teacher who has taken a small amount of time to study body language could be two or three times more effective in the classroom than a teacher who has just used the body language that he or she has picked up day by day through life. What is more, good and positive body language actually can make you feel a lot less stressed and a lot healthier.'

I am sure that all teachers would welcome any approach which could result in less stress. We can not expect this to happen, however, without there being a conscious effort to look at and copy certain aspects of effective body language. Again, Tony Attwood says: 'But remember, if you make body language just something of slight interest, you won't ever change. You really have to be determined to alter practices you have developed after years of habit'.

VITAL can provide a starting point for this. We can look at the body language of the teachers in VITAL and emulate it until it becomes quite natural for us. The strange thing about acting out positive behaviours is that they actually make you feel better. We probably all know the experience of talking ourselves into a bad mood: the more we feed ourselves with negative talk, the worse we feel. In a similar way we can influence our mood the other way by thinking positive thoughts and acting positively. Again, Tony Attwood has referred to the specific act of

..... and so finally John...... in conclusion ......I'm telling you ..... we really are going to have a good lesson together today!

smiling as an example of how deliberate, apparently mechanical acts can influence the way we feel: 'The implication of the research means that if we deliberately impose a false image of smiling upon ourselves then we will feel better, and our lessons will go better as well.' If we 'act out' being a positive and confident teacher, we begin to feel our confidence and effectiveness grow.

Be your own personal leader

Teaching is a job which demands a great deal of energy, and some teachers may argue that they haven't got the time to continually analyse their performance in the classroom. This is analogous to the lumberjack desperately trying to cut down trees with a blunt saw. When asked why he didn't stop to sharpen his saw he replied that he didn't have time to do that – he was too busy sawing! Reflection on teaching is important to all of us. Otherwise we may exhaust ourselves doing the job the hard, and perhaps least effective, way when a better solution is just around the corner. Maybe at times (if not all the time) we need to stop being busy, efficient *managers* in our classrooms and try to be our own *personal leaders*. We owe this to ourselves and to the pupils we teach. Stephen R. Covey, in his book *The Seven Habits of Highly Effective People*, gives clarity as to why it is important to have the qualities of leadership as well as management. He draws a distinction between leadership and management as follows:

You can quickly grasp the important difference between the two if you envision a group of producers cutting their way through the jungle with machetes. They're the producers, the problem solvers. They're cutting through the undergrowth, clearing it out.

The managers are behind them, sharpening their machetes, writing policy and procedure manuals, holding muscle development programs, bringing in improving technologies and setting up working schedules and compensation programs for machete wielders.

The leader is the one who climbs the tallest tree, surveys the entire situation, and yells, 'Wrong jungle!'.

But how do the busy, efficient producers and managers often respond? 'Shut up! We're making progress.'

Stephen R.Covey

There is a great deal of comfort to be had in being seen as a manager – someone who gets things done. And clearly there is a place for being a manager in the role of an effective classroom practitioner. But there is no credit to be had in doing something the long and less effective way if a better and more efficient solution is available.

Peter Drucker and Warren Bennis (cited in Stephen R. Corey: *The Seven Habits of Highly Effective People*) said:

> *Management is doing things right; leadership is doing the right things.*
>
> *Peter Drucker and Warren Bennis*

The more time we make available by carrying out tasks as leaders, the more time we have to devote our energies to other tasks essential for effective management in the classroom. In my opinion teaching is a hard enough job without unnecessarily wearing a hair shirt. Teachers who do this and run around appearing to be constantly busy and stressed may satisfy some inner need they have, but they may not be best servicing the needs of the pupils they teach. Stephen R. Covey says:

> *Effectiveness – often even survival – does not depend solely on how much effort we expend, but on whether or not the effort we expend is in the right jungle. And the metamorphosis taking place in every industry and profession demands leadership first and management second.*
>
> *Stephen R. Covey*

We must be aware that we need to rise above the demands of the immediate and, at times, above trivia, in order to advance as teachers. This links with the personal time management of a teacher, as referred to in the final paragraphs of this chapter.

We need to share our vast expertise

The Hay McBer Report highlights the need for teachers to share their good practice. It says:

> School managers will need to create a school climate that fosters a framework for continuous improvement. One critical dimension is likely to be openness to the integration of good practice from other teachers, regions or even countries.

Sharing good practice is what VITAL is all about. VITAL Stage 1 aims to share some of the characteristics of effective teachers in England. Stage 2 will add to this by looking at good practice in Spain and France.

I was heartened recently, whilst attending an EiC (Excellence in Cities) meeting in Leeds, by a headteacher at a 'Beacon school' in Leeds who spoke with incredible enthusiasm about the links she had made with another school in Leeds and how her school and teachers had benefited and learned so much from the 'partner' school. Partnership and sharing good practice should surely be what the 'Beacon school' initiative is about. The so called 'Beacon school' itself can learn as much from the partners it works with as the partners themselves. We can all learn. There is good practice in every school. The videos within the VITAL project simply show a number of effective teachers in action. My hope is that all teachers who watch this video will be able to learn something from what they see, and that this will act as a catalyst for further mutual sharing of good practice. The video can be viewed in the comfort of your own home, away from the immediate pressures of school, or in the context of some organized training concerning teaching and learning good practice within the school. It can then be used as a resource which will ideally promote discussion between colleagues in your own school, college or raising achievement division, among others.

Small things can be big things

If you feel that you cannot learn to be a better teacher then VITAL is not for you. On the other hand, there may be something, however apparently small, which could have a positive effect on your teaching. Throughout my own 18 years as a teacher I have become increasingly aware of how the sometimes simple things I can do (but maybe up until some point in my teaching have not done, for a variety of reasons) can make a tremendous difference to my teaching. The 'That's really good, I wonder why I haven't done that before' syndrome is certainly what I have experienced on a number of occasions. The small things can make a real difference. Bruce Barton expressed this with these words:

> *Sometimes when I consider what tremendous consequences come from little things ... I am tempted to think there are no little things.*
>
> Bruce Barton

What many teachers will think of as obvious good practice can easily be missed by others who have simply not thought about or encountered a particular technique. The same teachers, however, may themselves miss a number of 'obvious good practice' techniques used by others. I believe that any talk about certain aspects of classroom practice being common sense should be viewed with great caution – common sense is only a reality when it is familiar or a habit.

Be proactive and concentrate on the things you can change

Clearly, there are certain things which are beyond the control of the classroom teacher and these do impact on classroom effectiveness. These include:

- timetable constraints, with a teacher a nomad in the school, moving from one classroom to another
- the level of technical support provided – for computers, for example
- general levels of resources in the classroom
- the mood of pupils, caused by the baggage of problems they bring to school with them
- the time of day and the sequence of lessons within which you see your pupils.

If we simply react to these problems, however, and say that there is nothing we can do to rectify potential problems, then we cannot progress. Stephen R. Covey has drawn up a useful table of reactive and proactive words, which we may benefit from considering for a moment.

Reactive language	Proactive language
● There's nothing I can do.	● Let's look at our alternatives.
● That's just the way I am.	● I can choose a different approach.
● He makes me sound so mad.	● I control my own feeling.
● They won't allow that.	● I can create an effective presentation.
● I have to do that.	● I will choose an appropriate response.
● I can't …	● I choose …
● I must …	● I prefer …
● If only …	● I will …

It is a good idea to start using proactive language in general conversation. Linked with this is the way we face inevitable problems and setbacks in our lives as teachers. With regard to this Covey says:

> *It is not what happens to us, but our response to what happens to us that hurts us.*
>
> Stephen R. Covey

Teachers can be proactive and adopt a teacher-centred approach that accepts external limiting factors which are beyond their control and then seeks solutions. This is what effective teachers do. The teachers in VITAL do this. Tony Attwood has recently written that by adopting effective teaching and learning strategies it is possible to improve the grades of pupils by as much as two GCSE grades. If there is truth in this (and I believe there is) then it is surely not an option for any teacher not to analyse what he or she does in the classroom and be open to the challenge of learning new skills. As with all aspects of life, putting a bit of effort into being more proactive can ultimately make our work easier.

> *The point is that although we may feel as if we are doing everything we can, and feel that any other work would be impossible, these feelings may not be a valid measurement of reality. It may be that we could each of us teach more effectively with less effort.*
>
> Tony Attwood

Teachers may say, 'Can this be possible? Is it right to think this in teaching? Can this really be good for us?' I am not suggesting that we should put less effort into what we do, but rather that being more proactive liberates us to ensure that the effort we expend is more focused and directed towards really influencing our pupils' progress. Efficiency through being proactive is equally valid in teaching as in any other walk of life.

Aim to enjoy teaching – it's good for you and good for your pupils

It is vitally important for teachers to continue to enjoy what they do. I believe this is best done by setting personal challenges, whether they are big or small. We all need to feel there is something that we can aim for – a personal 'target', if you like (though I hesitate to employ this word that is so overused in teaching!). Recently a programme on the BBC looked at what made people happy, and specifically looked at very wealthy people – some, in fact, who had recently won the National Lottery. A lady on the programme said that she had felt very depressed with the amount of wealth she had until she found a challenge. The challenge she found was to help people. By giving to others she found that she was able to see great purpose in her life. This is of course a very well accepted idea – and one which forms a central part of many religions. A lot of teachers express the idea that a great part of the attraction of teaching is the sense that it is a caring profession, coupled with the feeling of giving pupils something which is of great importance in their life. It is only possible to really give a great deal, however, when one is feeling mentally and physically fit. In the case of teaching this doesn't imply that we all have to be like top-class athletes, but rather, invigorated by the experience of teaching. The aim should be to find as much enjoyment in teaching as in the things one does in one's spare time. I know that to some teachers who are feeling particularly stressed this will sound preposterous, but it should be an aim for all of us.

The continuing need for effective teachers will not decrease with modern technology

One thing that has struck me whilst making VITAL is how important the role of an effective teacher still is to the good atmosphere in a classroom and the effective progress of pupils. The recent Hay McBer Report made this clear and although it may seem obvious (again, some would say it is 'common sense') it needs to be emphasized. There is no doubt that in the changing world we are entering, information technology will significantly impact on the experience of pupils in schools. As is already happening, the concept of the traditional lesson will change for many pupils, with the techniques for delivery being modified and enhanced. Pupils will, for example, be able to access lessons that have been pre-recorded and dip into these in a progressive and, at times, individual way. As I watched the VITAL teachers, however, I did question in my own mind how this could ever replace the multisensory experience (the smells, the temperature, the ambiance, etc.) that pupils receive in traditional lessons. How could these things ever be easily captured electronically? I don't want to appear to be a Luddite in this respect, because I am very excited by the opportunities for improved learning experiences which IT offers. Nevertheless, a teacher's ability to effectively communicate, to have the respect of her pupils and to inspire confidence through her enthusiasm will always be a precious commodity. As human beings we all need the personal ingredient provided by interaction other individuals.

Construct a lesson in the correct way

To a certain extent an analogy can be drawn between teaching and cooking. Just as it is important in cooking to have the right ingredients, to use the right amount of each of them, and to use them in the correct order, so in teaching – the things we do in the classroom, the amount of each thing we do, and the order in which we do them are significant for an effective learning environment. An effective teacher often struggles to explain what he does to make his lessons effective, just as a cook who instinctively knows what to do may struggle to say precisely how he creates a gourmet masterpiece. In teaching this must be something that is overcome so that all teachers can begin to use the same language to describe the factors which go to make an effective teacher. What we do know is that when a teacher uses the right ingredients in a lesson but in the wrong order or in the wrong quantities, the result will always be disappointing.

In VITAL you need to decide what you think is important to you and throw away anything which you think wouldn't work for you. My only request would be for you to give things a go before you discard them – you never know, one of these things might just be an important classroom tool which proves to be very useful.

The quality of a teacher's performance is the quality of their communication

> … the quality of your life is the quality of your communication.
>
> *Anthony Robbins*

If this is true then the importance of being a good communicator cannot be more important in any walk of life than in teaching. John Freeman, the adviser I have worked closely with on this project, says that most teachers tend to do too much talking in their lessons. It is therefore essential that what we do say is carefully considered. Again, Anthony Robbins believes that a key skill of highly successful people is their ability to create rapport. It is not necessary to have a natural gift in order to do this. What is important is to listen to what pupils say and watch what they do in order to enter into a sense of rapport. This is not to say that we should behave like children but rather, respond to the ways they view life and therefore learning. Pupils often have a completely different view of life to a teacher and therefore find it hard to respond to the slant on life that the teacher represents to them. Good teachers can empathize to some extent with the views of pupils in order to engage them fully in the work they are doing.

Focus on success

All theories in education, of course, need to be balanced against the reality of life in the classroom. It can drain, tire and, at times, emotionally strain every nerve fibre in your body. As teachers we sometimes torture ourselves with dark thoughts and reflections on the failure of one lesson, even when this was in the middle of a series of other, highly effective lessons. We tend then to question our skill as a teacher, and if this develops into a circle of persistent worry it can be highly destructive. VITAL is about reflecting on what we do, but with the aim of improving, which includes looking at what we do well. We must always remember and applaud ourselves for our successes.

Recently Sue Cowley, author of *Starting Teaching: How to Succeed and Survive*, said:

Finally, a tip for when you're tearing your hair out and everything is going wrong. Take a step back, and react from your head instead of your heart. Don't respond to poor behaviour emotionally, by blaming yourself and becoming stressed. Instead, view the situation intellectually. Even the most experienced teacher finds some students and some classes hard to deal with.

Sue Cowley

Tomorrow really is another day!

Most teachers are over-critical of themselves. They tend to dwell on examples of less effective lessons and forget the successes they have experienced. I suspect all teachers have experienced this – I certainly have. The surprising thing is that you wake up the following day and the failures of yesterday can be replaced by great successes. We should all perhaps take on board the simple philosophy of Margaret Mitchell in *Gone With the Wind*, who said in 1936: 'After all, tomorrow is another day'. I certainly have to remind myself of this continually.

And just as we, as teachers, feel the great need to experience success, so, clearly, do pupils. Thomas Wolfe once said:

There is nothing in the world that takes the chip off one's shoulder like the feeling of success.

Thomas Wolfe

Any teacher will echo this; and it also applies to pupils. When pupils who are used to being given feedback of failure receive a sense of success, their whole persona suddenly changes. They are lifted, they are rejuvenated, and they are suddenly filled with optimism. The chip on their shoulder is suddenly removed. This is why giving sincere praise and positive feedback to pupils is so necessary. Some people have said that any negative comment ought to be balanced by at least five positives. This is a good starting point on the learning curve to giving positive feedback as a teacher. Eventually, however, praise will become the norm. This is not to say that pupils should not be told when they do things that are inappropriate. This is, in fact, essential. What is important, however, is to have a general classroom atmosphere that is positive, constructive and imbued with growth.

As I have suggested, it is my belief that we must always strive to improve – there is always something new to be learned. As long as this is the case we should not punish ourselves when things don't go as well as we would have liked. It is vital that we always remember our successes, whilst being prepared to think and try to correct any difficulties encountered. The very act of thinking is not always easy. But thinking is essential if we are to appreciate fully what we have achieved, what we are successful at, and what we need to work on to improve. Henry Ford expressed the problem people have with thinking:

> *Thinking is the hardest work there is, which is the probable reason why so few engage in it.*
>
> *Henry Ford*

As teachers, it is essential that we think and review our performance on a regular basis.

Believe in yourself

Emerson said:

> *What you are shouts so loudly in my ears I cannot hear what you say.*
>
> *Ralph Waldo Emerson*

To be aware of this is so important for us as teachers. Children all have PhDs in psychology, and will determine immediately the intentions of a teacher. 'Is he fair?' 'Is she firm?' 'Can I trust her?' 'Does he want the best from me?' All these things children will form views on very quickly. If a teacher's intention is not right, they will detect this immediately.

Sometimes when a class or pupil is causing a teacher problems, a conscious paradigm shift is of great benefit. Simply constantly holding a paradigm (or a belief or perception) of a class or a pupil as a problem often makes a teacher enter the class with the wrong intention. We have all been there and done that. The trouble is that the class or pupil will then sense that you expect them to misbehave, and the dance will then begin, with both the teacher and the class/pupil knowing the sequence of steps that will follow.

Research apparently shows that people who are effective in whatever walk of life are able to visualize and feel what they are going to do before they do it. I have heard Sally Gunnell say that she pictured precisely how she would run the 400m hurdles race before she set out. It is important for teachers to visualize success in the classroom. If you see yourself as having problems, you will have problems. If you struggle with a positive visualization of yourself in the classroom, then watch the teachers in VITAL, adopt some of their tactics and use these as part of your personal positive visualization. Practising some of the things the teachers in VITAL do (however apparently trivial to begin with) will seem like an act to begin with. But once they have been tried on a number of occasions and been found to be successful they will be internalized and become a habit.

> *Pupils all have PHds in psychology. They sense weaknesses at one hundred paces. This is why, through consideration and learning of techniques, we owe it to ourselves to be at least one step ahead.*
>
> Tony Swainston, 2001

PHds in Innocence Studies and Applied Analysis of Teacher Control Susceptibility

Effective time management

Stephen R. Covey gives a matrix which I have found useful as a way of looking at effective time management. Essentially he defines activities as:

A   important and urgent

B   important but not urgent

C   not important but urgent

D   not important and not urgent

I understand *urgent issues* as things we feel we must do – certainly other people are often happy to see us do these things. They can also be fairly pleasant, easy or rather mechanical to accomplish, but often not really important. So what is meant by 'important'?

Important issues are those things which, when accomplished, can have long-term benefits and contribute to your personal mission or the mission of the school. They match your deep values and the goals you have set yourself.

Looking at the matrix overleaf, Covey says that we often focus too much on the Segment A activities. He terms these 'crisis' activities. We can spend so much time on these activities that we find that when we are not doing them, we often escape into Segment D activities as a means of escape.

Some people spend a lot of time carrying out Segment C activities, thinking they are actually carrying out Segment A activities. They are often driven by the requirements of others and think that the things they are doing are important, when in reality there could be a far better way of completing this work – if indeed it needs doing.

The thing we should aim to do is to enter into Segment B activities as much as we can. These are the activities that nurture us and can have a long-term benefit for us, as well as our role as classroom practitioners. Some teachers will argue that they don't have enough time to enter this zone. But the alternative is to be driven by circumstances without looking to the opportunities that exist. The choice is between:

A being reactive and being driven by external influences; and

B being proactive and looking to shape what the future will look like.

I am aware that there is value to be had from Segment D ('not important and not urgent' zone). As it says in this segment, these can be pleasant activities – and what is wrong with that? Nothing really, as long as there is enough time left to carry out the crucial work in Segment B ('important but not urgent').

What you put in these categories (segments or zones) will be up to you. I know I have discussed, argued, and disagreed to some extent with my wife (who also teaches) on what they should contain. I have simply put certain things down in the matrix below for your guidance. However, the process of doing this for yourself is, I believe, very important. I would therefore recommend that you fill in your own matrix in the blank table provided below.

	URGENT	NOT URGENT
IMPORTANT	**SEGMENT A** ● teaching/preparing lessons ● essential marking of books ● writing reports ● parents' evenings ● registers ● departmental/pastoral meetings ● assemblies	**SEGMENT B** ● considering new teaching and learning styles ● considering new behaviour management techniques ● considering rewards and punishments ● keeping up to date with new ideas in education
NOT IMPORTANT	**SEGMENT C** ● responding immediately to certain requests of pupils and others ● some photocopying ● reacting to (or 'dealing with') certain aspects of misbehaviour ● responding immediately to certain phone calls	**SEGMENT D** ● general trivia ● time wasters ● cup of tea in the staffroom ● responding to a minor phone call ● some phone calls ● pleasant activities

(Adapted from Stephen R. Covey, *The Seven Habits of Highly Effective People*)

My time management matrix

	URGENT	NOT URGENT
IMPORTANT		
NOT IMPORTANT		

You may wish to photocopy the blank table and fill it in for future reference with your own present ideas. It may then be useful to refer back to it periodically to see if you are beginning to spend more time in Sector B ('important but not urgent'). The importance of rising above the immediate to see the long-term goal is well worth while. As Benjamin Disraeli said: 'Little things affect little minds'.

We must all try to be teachers who effectively and efficiently deal with the little things which face us in teaching, so that we can spend time concentrating on the things which may not be urgent – but are in the long term critically important.

Final thoughts

With each of the teachers in VITAL I have given my views on what I believe makes them effective teachers. The importance of looking at the evidence is really to come up with your own conclusion and views. You may therefore wish to look at the teachers first and then read my analysis. You may well disagree with a lot, or perhaps all, of what I say. I believe the process of watching the teachers is more important than it is for everyone to reach the same conclusions.

The important thing for teachers is to keep on learning throughout our careers. Teaching should be viewed as a research-based profession – whether the research is on a large or personal, small scale. We can always learn from new ideas – we should always be willing to look, ask questions and learn. The following quotes referring to the theme of continually asking and enquiring may provide you with some inspiration – and you may indeed wish to display some of them around your classroom.

> *Anyone who stops learning is old, whether at twenty or eighty.*
>
> *Henry Ford*

> *The fool wonders, the wise man asks.*
>
> *Benjamin Disraeli*

> *All men by nature desire knowledge.*
>
> *Aristotle*

> *I do not think much of a man who does not know more today than he did yesterday.*
>
> *Abraham Lincoln.*

> *Knowledge is the antidote to fear.*
>
> *Ralph Waldo Emerson*

> *The important thing is not to stop questioning.*
>
> *Albert Einstein*

> *He who asks is a fool for five minutes, but he who does not ask remains a fool forever.*
>
> *Old Chinese saying*

> *Not to know is bad; not to wish to know is worse.*
>
> *African Proverb*

Being proactive allows a person to be efficient, to be in control and to do the job better. A lot of the wasted time and effort caused by continually reacting to situations and crises without a thoroughly analysed understanding of the best way of dealing with them can be removed by being proactive. The table or matrix above is a useful way of analysing your present time allocated to being proactive and, as a result, a useful incentive for consciously thinking about making a shift where necessary.

Good luck – and I hope you enjoy watching the teachers in VITAL Stage 1 as much as I enjoyed putting this part of the project together.

Summary of the Hay McBer Report

A Model of Teacher Effectiveness. Report by Hay McBer to the Department for Education and Employment – June 2000' looks at the effectiveness of teachers by dividing the analysis up into three key elements. These are:

1   Teaching skills
2   Professional characteristics
3   Classroom climate

All of these things are within teachers' control and significantly influence pupil progress.

Teaching skills

The Report sub-divides teaching skills into seven categories, as follows:

A	High expectations
B	Planning
C	Methods and strategies
D	Pupil management/discipline
E	Time and resource management
F	Assessment
G	Homework

These are similar to the Ofsted inspection headings. In addition to these seven categories, Hay McBer says that teaching skills can be observed in broad terms by:

● the way the lesson is structured and flows

● the number of pupils on task through the course of the lesson.

Professional characteristics

The report subdivides professional characteristics into five clusters, as follows:

	Cluster	Characteristics
A	Professionalism	• Challenge and support • Confidence • Creating trust • Respect for others
B	Thinking	• Analytical thinking • Conceptual thinking
C	Planning and setting expectations	• Drive for improvement • Information seeking • Initiative
D	Leading	• Flexibility • Holding people accountable • Managing pupils • Passion for learning
E	Relating to others	• Impact and influence • Teamworking • Understanding others

Referring to the clusters of professional characteristics, the Hay McBer Report says that effective teachers need to have some strengths in each of them. The report however, recognizes the distinctive qualities of each teacher, and makes clear that effective teachers show distinctive combinations of characteristics that result in success for their pupils. All effective teachers achieve success in a unique way with their own individual emphasis on certain professional characteristics more than others.

Classroom climate

The report subdivides 'classroom climate' into nine dimensions as follows:

A	Clarity	Clarity around the purpose of each lesson. How each lesson relates to the broader subject, as well as clarity regarding the aims and objectives of the school.
B	Order	Order within the classroom, where discipline, order and civilized behaviour are maintained.
C	Standards	A clear set of standards as to how pupils should behave and what each pupil should do and try to achieve, with a clear focus on higher rather than minimum standards.

D	Fairness	The degree to which there is absence of favouritism, and a consistent link between rewards in the classroom and actual performance.
E	Participation	The opportunity for pupils to participate actively in the class by discussion, questioning, giving out materials, and other similar activities.
F	Support	Feeling of emotional support in the classroom, so that pupils are willing to try new things and learn from mistakes.
G	Safety	The degree to which the classroom is a safe place, where pupils are not at risk from emotional bullying, or other fear-arousing factors.
H	Interest	The feeling that the classroom is an interesting and exciting place to be, where pupils feel stimulated to learn.
I	Environment	The feeling that the classroom is a comfortable, well organized, clean and attractive physical environment.

The Hay McBer Report says that teaching skills and professional characteristics are factors that relate to what a teacher brings to the job. A distinction between the two is drawn as follows: 'Whilst teaching skills can be learned, sustaining these behaviours over the course of a career will depend on the deeper seated nature of professional characteristics.'

The report describes the nature of professional characteristics as follows:

Professional characteristics are deep-seated patterns of behaviour which outstanding teachers display more often, in more circumstances and to a greater degree of intensity than effective colleagues. They are how the teacher does the job, and have to do with self-image and values; traits, or the way the teacher habitually approaches situations; and at the deepest level, the motivation that drives performance.

Classroom climate is referred to as an output measure: it is what the teacher creates through teaching skills and professional characteristics, and it is what influences the pupils to learn.

As I have indicated, The Hay McBer Report comfortingly says that teachers are not clones and that there are a number of ways for a teacher to achieve effectiveness.

There is, in other words, a multiplicity of ways in which particular characteristics determine how a teacher chooses which approach to use from a repertoire of established techniques in order to influence how pupils feel.

This overview of the Hay McBer Report is useful because in each of the analyses of the teachers in VITAL there will be reference to those factors in the report which apply to the observed effectiveness of the teachers. Five of the seven teaching skills (excluding only 'Assessment' and 'Homework') are highlighted in the analyses of the VITAL teachers. All five of the 'professional characteristics' clusters, and 15 of the 16 associated characteristics, are highlighted. (The only characteristic not linked with one of the VITAL teachers is 'understanding others'.

In the analysis of each teacher I have not referred to the 'classroom climate' dimensions because these are what the Hay McBer Report says result from the teaching skills and professional characteristics. You will no doubt be able to see a number of 'classroom climate' dimensions for yourself in each of the lessons shown, if you wish to do this.

The following quote from the report indicates that the time has come for us to look at other teachers and how they create a positive classroom climate, whilst at the same time being open to comments and suggestions about the classroom climate we ourselves create:

Despite the demonstrable impact of classroom climate on student motivation and performance, it is rare for British teachers, or teachers in other countries, to receive structured feedback on the climates they help create in their classroom.

Effective teachers – happy pupils: analyses of the teachers in VITAL

In the following I have picked out some of what I have called the *key elements* in the classroom management of each of the five British teachers in VITAL. The key elements are my initial thoughts on what elements contribute to making an effective teacher. Again, as I have said before, you may well consider yourself that there are other key elements more important than those I have chosen. You may also feel that some of the key elements I have identified in one teacher appear in, or are more relevant to, another teacher. This will almost certainly be the case. The process of deciding in your own mind what the 'key elements' are is what is most important in studying the VITAL teachers.

In addition I have looked at each teacher in terms of the 'teaching skills' and 'professional characteristics' identified in the Hay McBer Report. Again, you will have your own view on which of the skills and characteristics are most evident in each teacher. What I have presented is more a framework showing examples of key elements, teaching skills or professional characteristics, rather than a complete and definitive set for each teacher. There will also be some overlap between the key elements I have identified and the teaching skills or professional characteristics identified in the Hay McBer report. I have indicated where I think that this is the case.

For each of the five teachers you will see a brief profile, which I hope will place the teaching of each one in a clearer context. In addition, there is an initial summary of the key elements, teaching skills and professional characteristics identified for each teacher.

Larraine Biscombe

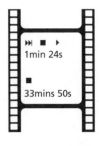

1min 24s

33mins 50s

...I give 100% to the pupils and I demand 100% from them... Preparation is the be-all and end-all.

Larraine Biscombe

VITAL Teacher Profile – Larraine Biscombe

Age:	51
Present school:	John Smeaton Community High
Number of pupils in the school:	Approximately 1600
Age range:	11 to 18
Age range I teach:	11 to 16
Date I joined my present school:	1992
Total years of teaching:	25
Previous schools:	Fir Tree Junior School Fir Tree Middle School Various schools on supply during time out from full-time teaching to raise a family!
Subjects I teach:	French PSHE
Year group taught in the VITAL video:	Year 8

Larraine Biscombe

Summary of key elements

The key elements are my initial thoughts concerning the characteristics that make Lorraine an effective teacher.

1	pupils immediately on task
2	positive body language
3	earning the respect of pupils
4	assertive use of the voice
5	the importance of the classroom environment
6	having a sense of humour
7	adopting a business-like approach with high expectations
8	using games and having fun
9	pupil movement
10	personal impact and presence

Direct links with the Hay McBer Report

Teaching skills

The teaching skill identified in Lorraine from the Hay McBer Report is:

■ Methods and strategies

Professional characteristics

The three professional characteristics identified in Lorraine from the Hay McBer Report are:

Cluster	Characteristic
A Professionalism	● confidence
C Planning and setting expectations	● initiative
D Leading	● managing pupils

Larraine Biscombe – key elements

Key element 1 – pupils immediately on task

The start of a lesson is a critical time in setting the tone for the work to be done. As soon as the pupils begin to enter Larraine's classroom they are on task in French. The period when pupils enter a classroom can present difficulties for a teacher. No one wants to begin a lesson by shouting at a class to be quiet, but this can happen if a class enters the room continuing their discussions from earlier on. Larraine's solution to this is to accept that pupils like to talk (to fill the silence vacuum!) and to use this to her advantage by getting them to chant numbers, dates, etc. as they enter the room and also during transitions between one activity and another.

There is often a period of dead time when pupils enter a classroom. It is, therefore, well worthwhile for a teacher to think about how to make this time more productive, and as a result start the lesson in a more efficient way. This will clearly not involve pupils chanting out numbers in every lesson – this particular technique to get the pupils quickly on task may not suit everyone's style. Simple things like having an instruction written on the board as they enter the classroom, which immediately gives the pupils a task to carry out, is often enough to transform a lesson.

Larraine also has a general policy of the pupils not taking out their books, pens, pencils, etc. at the start of a lesson. Her reason for this is that she believes this exercise can cause a lot of disruption so she prefers to get the class settled and go through the initial part of the lesson without the pupils needing to write anything down.

Key element 2 – positive body language

Larraine's body language says, without any need for words, 'I am in control, trust me'. The classroom is her domain. She walks around to all quarters of it – no place is in any way a no-go area. She shows great confidence in her interactions with the pupils, inviting them to come out to the front with her, for example, without there being any hint of silliness. Larraine uses skills she says she has learned from acting – but these have now become part of her natural repertoire. What was once an act is now a habit. Repeating a central theme of VITAL: we can all learn new skills in a similar way by mirroring or copying other teachers.

Key element 3 – earning the respect of pupils

Larraine's pupils clearly have a deep respect for her. As well as this being obvious from the video, I have witnessed it from walking around the school with Larraine on a number of occasions. She has built up a reputation over a number of years and pupils now know what to expect from her. This is not to say that she ever relaxes in her endeavour to maintain or improve on her standards. When a teacher starts to think she knows all there is to know, and therefore stops trying out new methods in the classroom, this is often the start of a decline in her effectiveness and the standards of teaching, learning and discipline that pupils experience.

Key element 4 – assertive use of the voice

When Larraine gives an instruction there is no doubt in her voice that she expects instant action. She has a very assertive manner which is simultaneously expressive and warm. Again, Larraine has learned to use her voice partly through her interest in acting skills. An understanding of the use of the voice is a critical element in acting skills, which I believe could very productively be used by teachers.

Key element 5 – the importance of the classroom environment

Larraine's room is full of displays of pupils' work and creations of her own. She has taken time over this and the pupils will immediately be aware that she cares about what she does. Caring is very important. It is inevitable that pupils themselves will not care about their work if the teacher appears to lack motivation and interest in teaching them.

Key element 6 – a sense of humour

During the lesson on video the class laughs along with Larraine. This is a great way of building up relationships. It is important that pupils see that their teacher has a sense of humour, as Larraine says in her interview. Laughter is a basic way in which all human beings interact and an excellent way of breaking the ice or eliminating tension.

Key element 7 – adopting a business-like approach with high expectations

Larraine demands a lot of her pupils in return for the time and effort she puts in. This creates an atmosphere where learning is seen as important and where a structured, business-like ethos prevails. This is no accident. Larraine plans her lessons with great care, from the structure of the work to be done and materials to be used, to the clothes she wears. This all results in an environment which is safe and peaceful whilst at the same time being conducive to effective learning. (Mentioning clothes may seem strange in terms of planning a lesson, but pupils pick up an impression through all their senses, and the image the teacher presents in terms of dress will undoubtedly influence their approach to the lesson. The semiotics, or signs and symbols, including the light level, the smell and the acoustics of a classroom which combine to influence the work of pupils, is worth some thought.)

Key element 8 – using games and having fun

Teaching should be fun! Robert Powell spends some time in his videos on *Whole Class Teaching* on the use of games, and how they can motivate pupils. Often when pupils are playing games they don't think they are working. Larriane uses card games, which the pupils are clearly actively involved in. They have fun and there is the added ingredient of looking to see who wins, which gives spice to the whole process and is a natural incentive for competitive youngsters.

Key element 9 – pupil movement

The pupils move around the classroom without any fuss. This is due to the way in which they have realized Larraine's expectations over a period of time. Again, no success comes by accident. Larraine deals with her pupils with a firm but fair manner which allows them to understand the expectations she has, and her to be confident in them and trust their behaviour and response to her. Once this process is started it will tend to develop with both teacher and pupils feeling nourished by the relationship which is developing.

Key element 10 – personal impact and presence

This attribute is mentioned in the DfEE document *National Standards for Headteachers*, which says that it is possessed and displayed by all successful and effective teachers.

As I have indicated here, Larraine makes a real personal impact in the classroom. Her significant presence operates to get the best from the pupils. Could all teachers learn to be like this? Well, I clearly believe that it is possible and this is a key part of VITAL. But desire is not enough – it does take effort, commitment and time.

Larraine Biscombe – direct links with the Hay McBer Report

Teaching skills

■ Methods and strategies

Two of the key questions the Hay McBer Report asks about 'methods and strategies' are:

> ● Does the teacher involve all pupils in the lesson?
> ● Does the teacher use a variety of activities / learning methods?

It is evident from the video footage that Larraine does both of these things. She uses a variety of question-and-answer techniques, she allows pupils to work through problems together on a variety of exercises and she listens and responds to the questions of all her pupils. The Hay McBer Report 'saw effective teachers doing a great deal of direct instruction to whole classes, interspersed with individual and small group work'. That is what we see Larraine doing on the video.

Professional characteristics

■ Confidence

Under 'professional characteristics' and within the cluster of **professionalism** the Hay McBer Report emphasizes the importance of *confidence*:

> Effective teachers believe in themselves and have the conviction to be ambitious: for the pupils, for the school, and for themselves. Self-confidence is also fundamental to challenging poor performance and bringing about step change. Effective teachers see themselves as, and act as, 'leading professionals'. They have the emotional resilience to deal with challenging pupils, and the stamina necessary for sustained contribution in the classroom. Being confident about personal skills and believing in the value of their work in what they know is a demanding job, helps teachers to have a strong sense of identity, and to set boundaries for themselves so they know what they can and should take on.

The video of Larraine clearly demonstrates that she has a lot of confidence in front of the class. Her confidence is exemplified by key elements such as:

- positive body language
- earning the respect of pupils
- assertive use of the voice

As teachers we will all face challenging situations with pupils who test our determination and skill. Referring to this, the Hay McBer Report says about teachers who demonstrate confidence:

> They have emotional resilience in dealing with challenging pupils and situations. They are able to keep calm.

■ Initiative

Under 'professional characteristics' and within the cluster of **planning and setting expectations** the Hay McBer Report emphasizes the importance of *initiative*:

> In addition to the careful planning of mainstream lessons and programmes of work, effective teachers think ahead. This enriches the curriculum and makes learning relevant and coherent.
> Alert, action-oriented teachers stand out, and command respect, with colleagues as well as pupils.

Larraine has a great presence in the classroom and around the school. She is very willing to take the lead and demonstrate initiative, demanding respect from both her colleagues and pupils. This is demonstrated through key elements such as:

- adopting a business-like approach with high expectations
- using games and having fun

■ Managing pupils

Under 'professional characteristics' and within the cluster of **leading** the Hay McBer Report emphasizes the importance of *managing pupils*:

> Takes action on behalf of the class. Speaks positively about the class to others and builds up its image. Goes out of his or her way to obtain the extra materials and resources the class, group or team needs: for example, by engaging the support of parents, the community or commercial organizations.

Larraine has a calm control of the pupils. Managing pupils effectively helps to create the right climate in the classroom and around the school. Larraine motivates every pupil, and gets them to move forward with her. She focuses their attention on the tasks they are required to do and she makes clear the learning objectives. The following key elements contribute to the way Larraine manages pupils:

- positive body language
- the importance of the classroom environment
- having a sense of humour
- pupil movement

In relation to managing pupils effectively, the Hay McBer Report mentions the need for effective teachers to have what we sometimes refer to as 'eyes in the back of their heads':

> Pupils in their classes will be aware of the 'lighthouse effect', the habitual scanning by which effective teachers appear to pick up everything that is going on.

Larraine demonstrates a great awareness of all that is going on in the classroom, even when groups are involved in very different group exercises at different stages of completion. She also gives very clear directions, gets all pupils quickly on task, and makes learning objectives very transparent to the class at all times, and particularly at the start and end of the lesson. The report refers to this as follows:

> They get pupils on task, clearly setting learning objectives at the beginning of a lesson and recapping at the end, and giving clear instructions about tasks.

Les Taggart

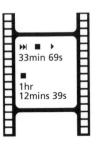

▸▸ ■ ▸
33min 69s

■
1hr
12mins 39s

They have got to learn by trying things ... that I don't have all the answers.

Les Taggart

VITAL Teacher profile – Les Taggart

Age:	47
Present school:	Benton Park School in Leeds
Number of pupils in the school:	Approximately 1400
Age range:	11 to 18
Age range I teach:	11 to 18
Date I joined my present school:	1975
Total years of teaching:	26
Previous schools:	None
Subjects I teach:	Physical education: core, GCSE and A'level
Year group taught in the VITAL video:	Year 8

Les Taggart

Summary of key elements

The key elements are my initial thoughts concerning the characteristics that make Les an effective teacher.

1	warmth of personality
2	clarity of instructions
3	a positive use of questions and answers
4	sincere praise
5	the use of kinaesthetic instructions
6	a sense of humour
7	use of the unexpected
8	entertainment as a learning tool.
9	congruence of messages
10	genuine enthusiasm
11	subject expertise
12	clear lesson structure
13	the use of the names of pupils
14	reliability and integrity

Direct links with the Hay McBer Report

Teaching skills

The teaching skill identified in Les from the Hay McBer Report is:

■ High expectations

Professional characteristics

The three professional characteristics identified in Les from the Hay McBer Report are:

Cluster	Characteristic
A Professionalism	● creating trust
C Planning and setting expectations	● drive for improvement
D Leading	● holding people accountable

Les Taggart: key elements

Key element 1 – warmth of personality

One of the things which I believe is instantly noticeable about Les is the warmth of his personality. It may be true to say that this is not something that is easy to mirror, but it is an undeniable strength in a teacher's toolkit. To some extent the warmth a teacher demonstrates can develop and flourish once he is confident in what he is doing. There is a clear symbiotic relationship between a teacher's warmth and his confidence: they nourish one another. However, like the TV newsreader who has to remain apparently calm and cool when the video footage fails to appear or the autocue she is reading from disappears, so a teacher must display calm in all circumstances in the classroom. This initial act of remaining calm will develop into something that becomes more natural when the teacher experiences the effectiveness of it. Calm control will become the norm, and warmth of personality will develop as a result. Les's relationship with his pupils has been built up over a number of years. Warmth within the classroom will bring respect from the pupils through the confidence they gain from the teacher. Pupil confidence will also develop from the following key element.

Key element 2 – clarity of instructions

Les issues instructions with clarity and gives his pupils confidence in the work they are doing with him. He adopts a central position in the gym and is always in full control of the group and the activity. His hand gestures are both reassuring and natural – but it is possible for anyone to copy these so that they become natural in appearance and, over a period of time, a 'habit'. He displays great confidence in his own ability and his right to be the teacher, but without any hint of an aggressive stance.

Following an activity, Les demonstrated a simple but very effective technique for getting the pupils to come to a standstill: the class is asked to do a jump-stop when he blows the whistle. This brings them immediately to a standstill ready for the next instruction. Teachers in classrooms (and also games teachers) sometimes find it hard to get pupils to stop one activity and receive the instructions for another. This can be a cause of great stress and it is important, no matter what technique is used, that pupils become familiar with the signal a teacher uses to get back their attention.

Key element 3 – positive use of questions and answers

Les uses questions and answers as a key element of the lesson. There are some people who claim that the use of direct questions by a teacher can be counterproductive, with only a few pupils actively participating in the process and others largely dissociated from the activity. I understand that this can indeed be the case when classes are either reluctant to answer questions for fear of being ridiculed by their peers, or when they are simply not interested and motivated by the prospect of answering questions. It clearly works in this situation for Les, however, and is a critical part of the way he conducts the lesson.

Key element 4 – sincere praise

A key element in the repertoire of any successful teacher is the use of praise. There is a rule of thumb that any negative comment directed at a pupil should be balanced by at least five positives. Les repeatedly gives positive feedback and encouragement. This succeeds as well as it does because it is *sincerely* given. The *intention* of a teacher is very important. In other words, if a positive comment is given, but does not match with what the class perceives as the real feelings of the teacher, then there is a lack of congruity. This will result in the class feeling uneasy with the mixed messages they receive.

Key element 5 – use of kinaesthetic instructions

Les employs a very kinaesthetic style in the way he carries out his lesson. He instructs the class by physically demonstrating the actions himself. Clearly, being a games teacher naturally involves more opportunities for the use of the kinaesthetic, but I would suggest that all teachers could learn from watching games teachers and incorporating their techniques into classroom based activities.

Key element 6 – a sense of humour

We all want to have a good time. Adolescents may at times give a different impression and their idea of a good time does not always match that of a teacher – or indeed their parents. But deep down we all want to be happy and content. The use of humour allows the class to see that the teacher is relaxed and comfortable with them – that he is indeed happy to be with them. Les demonstrates understated humour on a number of occasions and this undoubtedly adds to the general impression of control he has.

Key element 7 – use of the unexpected

This can be a useful way of constantly re-engaging puils' attention and keeping them wondering what will happen next. When you watch Les you will see that he subtly uses the unexpected to move the lesson along and maintain pupils' attention.

Key element 8 – entertainment as a learning tool

A good teacher will entertain a class. Again, this can be done in a variety of ways but it will significantly reduce the probability of a class becoming bored and as a result disruptive. A good teacher is a good performer – a good actor. The need for a teacher to be an actor was mentioned earlier and a number of the teachers in the VITAL project independently referred to acting skills as an important ingredient in the effectiveness of a teacher. Les naturally gives a good performance which constantly engages pupils' attention.

Key element 9 – congruence of messages

It is important that the different messages the pupils get from the teacher are matched, or congruent. If a teacher says one thing in words (e.g. 'Well done, John') but her tone of voice doesn't express that she is pleased with the work, then the pupil will get mixed messages and feel confused. What is said, how it is said, body language and facial expression should all match for the pupil to feel secure and confident. Les demonstrates congruence with each of these aspects.

Key element 10 – genuine enthusiasm

Les displays a genuine enthusiasm for the work he is doing with his pupils. A class will very rapidly pick up the message that the teacher is not particularly interested in the work they are doing. It is then little wonder if they respond by showing little enthusiasm themselves.

Key element 11 – subject expertise

Les demonstrates a good level of competence in the topic he is teaching. Clearly, a level of teacher expertise in the subject taught is useful. Some may say it is essential, and certainly in a number of subjects it is important that the correct facts are given. It is no good a teacher teaching about the Battle of Hastings in 1066 but getting the outcome of the battle wrong. In a similar way it no good a physics teacher going through the Theory of Special Relativity with a sixth form class without understanding the fundamental concepts herself. Due to timetabling commitments and constraints most teachers will have experienced teaching at times subjects which they are not so familiar with. As a result they will also have experienced the discomfort brought by pupils who ask questions and reveal the teacher's limited knowledge and understanding of the subject. With the inevitable changes brought about by information technology in the structure and content of lessons, teachers will at times have to adapt even more to not always knowing answers to the questions the class may ask. At times they will be on a journey of discovery with the class, which for some will be exciting and for others will present a new, threatening environment. Then the examples of effective teaching we are looking at in VITAL will be even more important.

Key element 12 – clear lesson structure

Les's lesson has a very clear progression throughout. There is no doubt that the pupils will have gained new knowledge and expertise by the end of the lesson, and in his interview on the video you will hear Les emphasizing the importance of all pupils achieving something. A teacher should always have clear aims and objectives for every lesson he teaches. Then he can set a series of challenges which all the pupils in the class can benefit from.

Key element 13 – using pupils' names

Les uses the names of pupils when he addresses them in the lesson. Getting to know the class is very important. The use of a person's name is a very powerful tool, and pupils will respond much better when the teacher uses their names and thus demonstrates an interest in them.

Key element 14 – reliability and integrity

This is mentioned in the DfEE document *National Standards for Headteachers*, which says that this attribute is possessed and displayed by all successful and effective teachers. Being reliable and a person of integrity perhaps sums up the general feeling one experiences when watching Les in action.

Les Taggart – direct links with the Hay McBer Report

Teaching skills

■ High expectations

One of the key questions the Hay McBer Report asks about 'high expectations' is:

> Does the teacher provide opportunities for students to take responsibility for their own learning?

Les gives very clear instructions, but within a framework that allows pupils to learn from their own experience, sometimes failing but always supported by positive correction and encouragement. The quote I have used at the beginning of this section on Les and taken from his interview shows how his views on this match those of the Hay McBer Report.

Professional characteristics

■ Creating trust

Under 'professional characteristics' and within the cluster of **professionalism**, the Hay McBer Report emphasizes the importance of *creating trust*:

> Being sincere and genuine creates an atmosphere of trust, and allows pupils to act naturally, express themselves honestly, and not be afraid of making mistakes – an essential starting point for learning. It also helps build rapport with pupils.

Les is sincere and genuine in his approach with the pupils. He is never patronizing but he demands high standards whilst allowing pupils to make mistakes and encouraging them to learn by trying. Les creates trust through key elements such as:

- warmth of personality
- clarity of instruction
- sincere praise
- the use of pupils' names
- reliability and integrity

■ Drive for improvement

Under 'professional characteristics' and within the cluster of **planning and setting expectations** the Hay McBer Report emphasizes the importance of the *drive for improvement*:

> This is about moving out of the comfort zone and providing challenge and excitement in the learning process.

The pupils Les teaches are clearly challenged and are stimulated by the learning environment he provides for them. Les talks in his interview about wanting all pupils, from the least to the most able, to be challenged by his lessons whilst feeling that they have all achieved something. This is very important because it is essential that pupils should feel a sense of achievement and that they can succeed. Pupils who feel that the challenge is too great will simply turn off, and this is often the cause of dissatisfaction and resultant discipline problems in a classroom. Les's emphasis on a drive for improvement permeates all he does and is exemplified by key elements such as:

● a clear lesson structure

■ Holding people accountable

Under 'professional characteristics' and within the cluster of **leading**, the Hay McBer Report emphasizes the importance of *holding people accountable*:

> Stating expectations and defining boundaries are needed in order to focus learning and minimize distraction. Clarifying accountability builds a sense of community with shared norms of behaviour. Clear and predictable routines create safety and security.

Safety and security are essential foundations for the lessons of any PE teacher – but this is true in all lessons. Without feeling safe and secure, pupils cannot learn. Les speaks with calm authority and there is little doubt that he expects high standards; and as a result this is what he and his pupils experience. Les creates a 'sense of community with shared norms of behaviour' through his interaction with the pupils. The following key elements are crucial in this:

● positive use of questions and answers

● a sense of humour

● congruence of message

● subject expertise

Neil Pointon

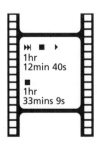

1hr
12min 40s

1hr
33mins 9s

I think I'm a bit of an actor, and I walk the plank each day.

Neil Pointon

VITAL Teacher Profile – Neil Pointon

Age:	52
Present School:	Roundhay School in Leeds
Number of pupils in the school:	Approximately 1400
Age range:	11 to 18
Age range I teach:	11 to 18
Date I joined my present school:	1988
Total years of teaching:	12
Previous schools:	None
Subjects I teach:	Chemistry Science Maths
Year group taught in VITAL video:	Year 10

Neil Pointon

Summary of key elements

The key elements are my initial thoughts concerning the characteristics that make Neil an effective teacher.

1	giving a number of degrees of freedom
2	closeness to the pupils
3	pupil respect
4	gentle and unthreatening guidance
5	warmth and humour
6	calling-out answers
7	a calm manner
8	knowing the pupils
9	adaptability to changing circumstances and new ideas

Direct links with the Hay McBer Report

Teaching Skills

The teaching skill identified in Neil from the Hay McBer Report is:

■ Planning

Professional characteristics

The three professional characteristics identified in Neil from the Hay McBer Report are:

Cluster	Characteristic
A Professionalism	● respect for others
B Thinking	● conceptual thinking
D Planning and setting expectations	● information seeking

Neil Pointon – key elements

Key element 1 – giving a number of degrees of freedom

The level of freedom allowed in a lesson is very important to the overall impact the lesson has on the pupils. Neil shows great confidence in giving a lot of responsibility and ownership for learning to the pupils. This allows the pupils to discover for themselves by a process of trial and error.

Key element 2 – closeness to the pupils

Neil's style involves him working closely on a one-to-one basis with pupils, answering their individual questions. His comments on the video about how he uses some of the skills he has learned from acting in his interactions with pupils are interesting and may be tried by other teachers.

Key element 3 – gaining the respect of pupils

Neil's pupils clearly like him. They respect his authority but they are confident enough to put forward their own views. Neil works with them through a negotiating style. 'We are working together' is implicit in all he does with the class. This requires a level of maturity from the pupils, but it can develop when they are given more ownership for their individual learning.

Key element 4 – gentle and unthreatening guidance

Neil employs a subtle style of mirroring the pupils to create empathy. He alludes to this in his interview and has gained these skills through experience and learning the skills of the actor. Through this approach he gives his pupils guidance without ever being dictatorial.

Key element 5 – warmth and humour

Neil demonstrates in all that he does that he likes working with his pupils. There is a warmth and a sincerity which they find comforting. Coupled with this is an underlying humour which breaks down any barriers that might otherwise exist.

Key element 6 – calling out answers

Neil allows the pupils to call out answers when they are around him at the end of the lesson. They do this with confidence and it eliminates the slower process of question/hand-up/selection of pupil/response from pupil/feedback on response from the teacher. It lets pupils feel they can answer questions more freely (they like to instantly call out a response) but it never gets out of control. This works well here and it is something to consider. A teacher could give the class a signal at times that they can just instantly give responses, whereas at other times putting up their hands first may be thought to be more appropriate. Variation and experimentation with these techniques is the important thing.

Key element 7 – a calm manner

Neil has a calm manner throughout the lesson. This gives pupils a feeling of being in a safe, structured and secure environment where learning can therefore flourish.

Key element 8 – knowing the pupils

Neil demonstrates that he knows his pupils very well. He says that this is something that he feels is crucial in his teaching. He knows who they are and what they are about and this assists the smooth running of his lessons. He uses their names and communicates with them on an intimate but, at the same time, controlled basis.

Key element 9 – adaptability to changing circumstances and new ideas

This is mentioned in the DfEE document *National Standards for Headteachers*, which says that this attribute is possessed and displayed by all successful and effective teachers. Neil demonstrates that he is willing to listen to the pupils' views and not be simply led by his own initial idea. Within the framework of a well-structured lesson, he therefore allows scope for growth, adaptability and development.

Neil Pointon – direct links with the Hay McBer Report

Teaching skills

■ **Planning**

Two of the key questions the Hay McBer Report asks about 'methods and strategies' are:

> ● Does the teacher have the necessary materials and resources ready for the lesson?
> ● Does the teacher review what the pupils have learned at the end of the lesson?

Neil's lesson has many elements to it in terms of what avenue of investigation the pupils may choose to go down. This has clearly got to happen within the framework of a well structured lesson in which there is a variety of equipment that the pupils can choose from. The materials and resources need to be available so that the lesson can flow. Flow in a lesson is very important, with different elements of the lesson knitting seamlessly together to make a coherent whole. Neil also makes a point of getting the pupils around him at the end of the lesson to review the findings in the lesson, the possible ways methods could be improved on and the successes the class has experienced.

Professional characteristics

■ Respect for others

Under 'professional characteristics' and within the cluster of **professionalism**, the Hay McBer Report emphasizes the importance of *respect for others*:

> Listening to others and valuing their contribution is fundamental to the empathy and exchange that is at the heart of education and learning.

This is an intrinsic part of Neil's negotiating style. He listens to what his pupils say and in some ways learns from them, as well as helping them. The Hay McBer Report mentions how a teacher who demonstrates respect for others helps pupils to become good citizens. This allows pupils to experiment, putting forward suggestions with confidence, and motivates them to succeed – perhaps far more than they ever believed possible. An open atmosphere of sharing views also helps pupils to develop a sense of community in the class and in the school. The Hay McBer Report also says:

> Respect for others underpins everything the effective teacher does, and is expressed in a constant concern that everyone should treat pupils and all members of the school community with respect.

The key elements which exemplify the way in which Neil shows respect for others include:

- giving a number of degrees of freedom
- pupil respect
- gentle and unthreatening guidance
- calling-out answers

■ Conceptual thinking

Under 'professional characteristics' and within the cluster of **thinking**, the Hay McBer Report emphasizes the importance of the drive for *conceptual thinking*.

> They therefore move easily between the big picture and the detail.

Encouraging pupils to endeavour to grasp concepts is often extremely difficult because it involves high-level thinking, and therefore can cause 'pain'. Grasping concepts can, however, be extremely fulfilling for both the pupils and the teacher. It requires the freedom for the individual to fail before succeeding, and this can only happen in a classroom environment which allows and values the views of individuals. Neil demonstrates how he often helps pupils to understand something very complex by gently guiding them and coaxing answers from them without directly and instantly giving them the answer. This will allow them to move from the detail to the 'big picture'.

Key elements which illustrate Neil's ability with pupils in this respect include:

- giving a number of degrees of freedom
- gentle and unthreatening guidance
- adaptability to new ideas and changing circumstances

■ Information seeking

Under 'professional characteristics' and within the cluster of **planning and setting expectations**, the Hay McBer Report emphasizes the importance of *information seeking*:

- ... having a deeper understanding of pupils, their background, who they are. And their prior learning and attainment helps teachers know what will interest and motivate them, so they can adapt their own approach. As a result, pupils are likely to feel recognized and valued as individuals.

- Finding appropriate resources and the best practise of others enhances teaching and learning, keeps approaches and programmes of work fresh, and avoids reinventing the wheel, ensuring effort is not wasted. Seeking out relevant inspection and research evidence can help improve planning and teaching.

The first statement defines an element that is absolutely crucial for an effective teacher. The more we can get to know our pupils, the more we will understand their needs and what influences them. We will also get to appreciate their particular preferred method of learning and therefore provide lessons which accommodate this. Neil talks in the interview about the importance of getting to know pupils, and in his interactions with them that we see on the video it is evident that he has a good grasp of each one as an individual.

The second statement is really what VITAL is all about. We must all be students or life-long learners wishing to find new and better ways of doing what we do – however effective we may already be. There is a vast amount of good practice which we can share and continually learn from each other as teachers. Neil mentions in his interview how he is always learning. Key elements which support Neil in this respect are:

- closeness to the pupils
- knowing the pupils

Phil Hardy

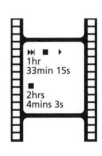

⏭ ■ ▶
1hr
33min 15s

■
2hrs
4mins 3s

❝*What I have learned is that it is much more effective to use positive measures and rewards rather than negative measures.*❞

Phil Hardy

VITAL Teacher Profile – Phil Hardy

Age:	44
Present School:	Crawshaw School
Number of pupils in the school:	Approximately 1150
Age range:	11 to 18
Age range I teach:	11 to 18
Date I joined my present school:	1984
Total years of teaching:	20
Previous schools:	Garforth Comprehensive
Subjects I teach:	History (Also Head of history and ITT coordinator)
Year group taught in VITAL video	Year 9

Phil Hardy

Summary of key elements

The key elements are my initial thoughts concerning the characteristics that make Phil an effective teacher.

1	involvement with the pupils
2	using pupils' names
3	showing respect for pupils
4	encouraging thinking
5	use of praise
6	having a sense of humour
7	enthusiasm for teaching
8	gaining the respect of pupils
9	commitment

Direct links with the Hay McBer Report

Teaching skills

The teaching skill identified in Phil from the Hay McBer Report is:

■ Pupil management/discipline

Professional characteristics

The three professional characteristics identified in Phil from the Hay McBer Report are:

Cluster	Characteristic
A Professionalism	● challenge and support
D Leading	● flexibility
E Relating to others	● teamworking

Phil Hardy – Key elements

Key element 1 – involvement with the pupils

Phil has a very close physical presence with the class. He achieves this when he is standing up and talking to the class by constantly moving around. Then, when the pupils are involved in group-work, he brings a warm and authoritative presence to all groups in the room. A teacher who always stands at the front of the class or, worse still, behind a desk, will appear to be afraid to enter into the province of the pupils – to be hiding behind a barricade. The classroom should be open in all areas with no 'no-go' areas for anyone – and certainly not the teacher.

Key element 2 – using pupils' names

I have referred to this with other teachers: the use of the pupils' names is such a simple but powerful tool. The truth of this is perhaps only really apparent when observing a teacher who does not use pupils' names.

It is very interesting to listen to politicians being interviewed on television or radio. They often use the name of the person they are interviewing and this immediately brings a sense of warmth and familiarity which helps the flow of the general discussion they are having. I think Tony Blair is a master at this, and deliberately uses this tool whenever he can, whether in an interview or talking to a member of the public. It may be argued that this is deliberate manipulation and just one part of the so called 'spin doctor' approach of the Labour Party, but the more relaxed and friendly feeling it engenders is hard to deny. Business people have also learned the value and power of using the Christian names of people they are talking to over the phone or face to face.

Our names are important to us – you only have to see the reaction of people when their names are spelt incorrectly or they are called by the wrong name, to understand this. Teachers who use the names of pupils will therefore have a real advantage in their interactions, whether in the classroom or around the school. The last thing a pupil wants when doing something they shouldn't be doing around the school is for a teacher to call out their name and ask them to come over. They feel far more secure and anonymous when the teacher has to resort to 'You, come over here', and indeed this can often be the trigger for the beginning of a long and potentially conflict-driven interaction between the teacher and pupil.

Key element 3 – showing respect for pupils

Phil's whole manner shows respect for his pupils. He refers to this as well in his interview:

> *I always respect pupils – every pupil I teach will always eventually be aware, through explicit or implicit means, that I respect them.*

When pupils give their responses and suggestions Phil is constantly feeding back praise. Showing respect for pupils will help to generate respect the other way. However difficult it may be, and as teachers we have all found situations where pupils have tested our altruistic emotions, we must dissociate the action of a pupil from the person themselves. In doing this we can show respect for the individual whilst being free to criticize their actions. Comments such as, 'You are a cheeky boy' will therefore just reinforce the behaviour which is being criticized. The pupil has been told he is cheeky, so he might as well continue to be cheeky in the future, and even in the present interaction with the teacher. Unless the teacher is lucky, a conflict spiral is therefore almost certain to develop. On the other hand, saying, 'The way you spoke just now is not appropriate, Susan. It's not what I expect from you,' is referring to an action – which the pupil can more readily accept, as it is not criticizing them as a person.

Key element 4 – encouraging thinking

A key part of the lesson shown here involves Phil eliciting the views of the class. This requires the class to think. Phil could have simply given the class the information, but getting them to think and come up with their own views is far more powerful as a teaching and learning tool. Thinking skills are now becoming a central part of the curriculum in many schools, with a growing understanding of the different ways that pupils can access information to enable them to comprehend work more effectively. Teachers often feel under pressure to get through the syllabus and an apparent simple way of achieving this is to didactically teach a class. Most teachers now realize, however, that this is not necessarily the best way to get pupils either to understand or to recall work.

Key element 5 – the use of praise

Phil gives this almost continuously – not in a casual way, but with sincerity and thought. His pupils, therefore, feel that they have earned their praise 'reward'.

Key element 6 – having a sense of humour

Another key tool in Phil's armoury is his sense of humour. I have referred to this with other teachers in VITAL and it really is an important part of a teacher's repertoire. Phil confirms this in his interview, and there is a central thread of humour throughout his entire lesson.

Key element 7 – enthusiasm for teaching

Like all effective teachers, Phil displays a real enthusiasm for teaching and a deep knowledge of his subject. He communicates this in a very down-to-earth-manner with pupils, using simple methods to stimulate them further. This may involve him simply saying things like 'That's three–nil, isn't it', when pupils volunteer their opinions. In doing this he is immediately sharing the lesson and the enthusiasm he has with the pupils.

Key element 8 – gaining the respect of pupils

The pupils obviously respect Phil. The main reason for this, I believe, is that they know that he cares about them and respects them. This is linked with all the other key elements already mentioned.

Key element 9 – commitment

This is mentioned in the DfEE document *National Standards for Headteachers*, which says that this attribute is possessed and displayed by all successful and effective teachers. Pupils know when the teacher is working for them and they will respond positively to this. Phil is clearly committed to developing as a teacher. He is also clearly committed to doing the very best for all the pupils he teachers.

Phil Hardy – direct links with the Hay McBer Report

Teaching skills

■ Pupil management / discipline
Two of the key questions the Hay McBer Report asks about 'Pupil management/discipline' are:

> ● Does the teacher treat praise good achievement and effort?
>
> ● Does the teacher treat different children fairly?

It is very clear from watching Phil that he does both of these things, as a natural and integral part of his lesson.

The Hay McBer Report says that highly effective teachers are able to 'create an environment in which all pupils can learn by employing direct means of pupil management to ensure that disruption to pupil learning is minimized and pupils feel safe and secure'. The 'lighthouse effect' in teaching is important, such that teachers are aware of everything that is going on around them in the classroom and that in addition they 'catch them being good' so that appropriate pupil behaviour is recognized and reinforced with praise.

Professional characteristics

■ Challenge and support
Under 'professional characteristics' and within the cluster of **professionalism** the Hay McBer Report emphasizes the importance of *challenge and support*:

> Expressing positive expectations of pupils – that they can and will learn and be successful – is one of the most powerful ways to influence pupils and raise achievement. It is one of the distinctive behaviours of high performing teachers who radiate confidence in their pupils and their potential, and never give up on them.

The report goes on to say:

> Effective teachers also provide **challenge and support** – a 'tough caring' where they not only cater for pupils' needs for physical and psychological safety but, crucially, repeatedly express positive expectations and build pupils' self-esteem and belief that they can succeed, as learners and in life.

Phil expects a lot of the pupils he teaches, and this gives them confidence to do well. When he refers to 'not expecting that kind of answer from a Year 9 pupil … that is GCSE standard', he boosts not only the confidence of the pupil he is referring to but also the class as a whole. He says this genuinely and with authority based on experience. It is well understood that pupils will only learn well when they are not anxious but rather comfortable and confident. Phil provides the comfort and confidence they need to grow as individuals. Giving pupils the feeling that they can succeed raises their self confidence and self-esteem.

Ways in which Phil challenges and supports pupils include the key elements:

- showing respect for pupils

- encouraging thinking

- the use of praise

■ Flexibility

Under 'professional characteristics' and within the cluster of **leading**, the Hay McBer Report emphasizes the importance of *flexibility*:

> Spontaneity generates vitality, helps to make it enjoyable, and may help growth of creative and imaginative approaches to problem-solving.

It is crucial that an effective teacher should be prepared to adapt to changing situations and change tactics when appropriate. What an individual pupil brings into the classroom can often stimulate a learning experience which an effective teacher will seize on. An effective teacher will react to pupil responses and take advantage of unexpected events.

Key elements which illustrate Phil's flexibility include:

- showing respect for pupils

- encouraging thinking

■ Teamworking

Under 'professional characteristics' and within the cluster of **relating to others**, the Hay McBer Report emphasizes the importance of *teamworking*:

> Teamwork between school colleagues, including support staff and others in the school community, is necessary to ensure an integrated and coherent approach that makes sense to pupils and facilitates their learning.

One of the roles Phil has in his school is that of being an ITT Coordinator. He refers in the interview to learning as much from the skills ITT students bring into the school as the students learn from their experience. Teaching is a life-long learning experience, and a great way of learning in a school is to operate as a team and benefit from the knowledge and experience of each individual. This encourages shared goals and greater effectiveness.

Mark Birch

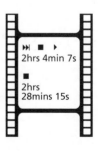

2hrs 4min 7s

2hrs
28mins 15s

 *There should never be a period when they are doing a task and they haven't been given a concrete time in which to perform it.*

Mark Birch

VITAL Teacher Profile – Mark Birch

Age:	30
Present school:	Benton Park School in Leeds
Number of pupils in the school:	Approximately 1400
Age range:	11 to 18
Age range I teach:	11 to 18
Date I joined my present school:	2000
Total years of teaching:	6
Previous schools:	Collenswood Comprehensive in Stevenage Garforth Community School in Leeds
Subjects I teach:	English
Year group taught in the VITAL video:	Year 9

Mark Birch

Summary of key elements

The key elements are my initial thoughts concerning the characteristics that make Mark an effective teacher.

1	the skills of an orator
2	relaxed body language
3	giving precise and specific instructions / references
4	good subject knowledge/expertise
5	praise / use of pupils' names
6	a sense of humour
7	making reference to youth culture
8	making reference to your own experience
9	create visual images
10	giving a time allowance for tasks
11	obvious enthusiasm and love of your subject
12	a clear structure and overall plan
13	intellectual ability

Direct links with the Hay McBer Report

Teaching skills

The teaching skill identified in Mark from the Hay McBer Report is:

■ Time and resource management

Professional characteristics

The three professional characteristics identified in Mark from the Hay McBer Report are:

Cluster	Characteristic
B Thinking	● analytical thinking
D Leading	● passion for learning
E Relating to others	● impact and influence

Mark Birch – key elements

Mark's style shown in this video-evidence is very individual and some may argue that it would be hard to mimic unless a storytelling approach is part of your repertoire. As I have indicated previously, however, I believe that it is possible to try out any different kinds of approach, and learn from everyone observed. The key is to mirror another teacher's style until it becomes part of your nature or a 'habit'.

Key element 1 – the skills of an orator

One of Mark's tools, which he uses very successfully here, is that of an orator. There can be a danger in teaching that too much talking is done by the teacher – John Freeman, as an adviser in Leeds over a number of years, says that this is perhaps his greatest general criticism of teachers. The voice, however, is clearly one of the chief ways of communicating, and just as the quality of our life is the quality of our communication, so the quality of our teaching depends significantly on our ability to verbally communicate with clarity. Mark not only speaks with clarity but he is also a good storyteller. The skills of an orator have an important role in engaging the imagination of pupils in teaching. Any teacher who has experienced having the class in the palm of their hand as they relate some experience or explain a certain concept will know the power of the delivery of words.

Key element 2 – a relaxed body language

Mark displays great confidence through his body language. He looks totally comfortable with his place in the classroom as the teacher, and this gives the pupils confidence. This, and the skills of orator, are clearly essential ingredients in the toolkit of an actor. Just as actors are trained and tutored in these skills, so I believe there is a place for them in education for teachers. A later VITAL project will concentrate wholly on the way in which acting skills can be learned and employed by teachers.

Key element 3 – giving precise and specific instructions / references

Mark gives the class an early indication of why the work they are doing is important. He refers directly to their SATS, and specifically mentions 'Section C of Paper 1', for example. The pupils know, therefore, that success in what they are about to do will pay dividends in something which is important to them. This class is an able group and Mark's pitch of the lesson suits their ability. All classes, however, should be engaged in work by understanding the importance of what they are doing. None of us like to do work in which we have no investment. Pupils are, of course, no different in this respect. (The same idea of investment applies to their behaviour. Pupils only misbehave when the attention they receive for doing so pays more dividends than the dividend they receive for their investment in good behaviour.)

Key element 4 – good subject knowledge / expertise

Mark is clearly very comfortable with his subject knowledge. Pupils will sense this and it will of course give them confidence. A teacher who is an expert in his subject will tend to be more flexible and receptive to the demands of individuals and different classes.

Key element 5 – praise / use of pupils' names

Like Les, Mark gives out a lot of *praise*. All effective teachers do this. Because they receive praise pupils are also given the confidence necessary to contribute their own views – and again, positive aspects of their contributions can be highlighted and rewarded with praise. When talking to his pupils, Mark uses their names. Our names are important to all of us as human beings. Like all of us, pupils will respond more positively to being referred to by their names rather than impersonal pointing or 'you'.

Key element 6 – a sense of humour

Having a sense of humour doesn't imply that a teacher should be telling jokes all the time – though a well-thought-out joke in the context of a lesson can be a very powerful motivator. Mark, however, employs humour in a number of subtle ways. He talks about 'bed to bed' stories, uses an unusual voice and refers to things as being 'so dull'. All of this helps the pupils to relate to him as an individual. These things seem so simple, but like all good practice in classroom management they are vital ingredients.

Key element 7 – making reference to youth culture

This is another way of relating to pupils. Mark uses references to Robbie Williams and his new video *Rock DJ*, which the pupils will immediately associate with. (At the moment Robbie Williams is popular and up-to-date, but perhaps by the time you read this he will be a little more dated!) Pupils will immediately think, 'Oh, he knows about this', and see the teacher more as an individual! Mark also relates to both boys and girls through the use of humorous stereotypical stories. (Teachers must always be wary of offending pupils, or indeed anyone else, by what they say. But a bit of common sense and knowing your audience allows you to feel freedom to talk in a professional and open manner to a class.)

Key element 8 – making reference to your own experience

Mark refers to incidents and experiences from his own life. He makes reference to 'my mate Dave's sister' and the urban myth. The effect this has is, again, that the class will be able to relate to him more as an individual.

Key element 9 – create visual images

This links with earlier comments about Mark using his skills as an orator in the lessons. Mark uses his body and movement to bring life to the story he is telling. Small movements and uses of the body can bring a visual aspect to parts of a lesson which otherwise may be predominantly an auditory experience.

Key element 10 – giving a time allowance for tasks

Mark mentions in his interview that he gives pupils a specific time to complete tasks. This is demonstrated in the classroom evidence on video when he gives the class three minutes to complete a task. The advantage of giving time allowances is that:

- pupils have a target for completing the work
- pupils don't have the time to be diverted into idle conversation
- pupils learn to work to specific deadlines

Key element 11 – obvious enthusiasm and love of your subject

Some people may have a tremendous knowledge of their subject but fail to enthral their pupils because they themselves seem to lack enthusiasm. Mark brings a fresh enthusiasm to his teaching, which will naturally inspire the pupils he teaches.

Key element 12 – a clear structure and overall plan

In the lesson shown on the video there is a very clear start, middle and end. There is also no doubt that the pupils will have learned some valuable skills concerning essay construction by the time they leave the lesson – I certainly did by watching Mark!

Key element 13 – intellectual ability

This is mentioned in the DfEE document *National Standards for Headteachers*, which says that this attribute is possessed and displayed by all successful and effective teachers. I believe that this does not just mean a simple and narrow measure of a teacher's IQ. Rather, I believe it is a conscious awareness of all the multiple-intelligences which teachers can draw on in themselves and also utilize with the pupils to produce a rich learning experience. Intelligence in the teacher therefore includes an understanding of preferred learning styles together with an appreciation of the emotional intelligence of individuals. (A good book for teachers to read concerning this is *Emotional Intelligence* by Daniel Goleman).

Mark Birch – direct links with the Hay McBer Report

Teaching skills

■ Time and resource management

One of the key questions the Hay McBer Report asks about time and resource management is:

> Does the teacher structure the lesson to use the time available well?

This clearly relates to the key element of a clear structure and overall plan.

It is evident from the video that Mark manages the class by having a clear structure for the lesson. This enables him to be relaxed and confident. The Hay McBer Report talks about there being over 90% of pupils on task with highly effective teachers. In Mark's lesson the pupils are eager to do the work and come up with their own individual contributions.

Professional characteristics

■ Analytical thinking

Under 'professional characteristics' and within the cluster of **thinking**, the Hay McBer Report emphasizes the importance of *analytical thinking*.

> Thoroughness in preparation, based on an accurate assessment of the stage pupils have reached–for the lesson, the term and the year–creates a framework for teaching and learning.

Effective lesson preparation takes into account the prior knowledge, understanding and ability of pupils. Mark outlines at the beginning of the lesson the purpose of the work and how it fits into other work they have so far covered. The Hay McBer Report emphasizes the need for milestones to be specified 'so that pupils have a sense of progress and can measure their own achievements against learning objectives'.
The report also suggests that by showing an analytical approach themselves, teachers will encourage pupils to adopt a logical approach and as a result question what and why they are doing things.

■ Passion for learning

Under 'professional characteristics' and within the cluster of **leading**, the Hay McBer Report emphasizes the importance of the *passion for learning*:

> ... the drive and an ability to support pupils in their learning, and to help them become confident and independent learners

A teacher who demonstrates the importance of a passion for learning introduces pupils to independent learning skills which allows them to become life-long learners. Such a teacher encourages pupils to work out answers for themselves. The following key elements are important in ensuring this:

● good subject knowledge / expertise

● obvious enthusiasm and love of your subject

● a clear structure and overall plan

■ Impact and influence

Under 'professional characteristics' and within the cluster of **relating to others** the Hay McBer Report emphasizes the importance of *impact and influence*:

> ... does something that will make learning vivid or memorable. Consciously manages pace in a lesson to maximize learning outcomes.

This links with the following key elements identified in Mark:

- making reference to youth culture
- making reference to your own experience
- create visual images
- good subject knowledge / expertize
- obvious enthusiasm and love of your subject

Showing an enthusiasm for the subject encourages pupils to share that enthusiasm. The effective teacher will use a range of techniques to accomplish this, and as a result the pupils will want to be there and enjoy learning.

Section Six

Using the extended video highlights

The extended video highlights show approximately thirty minutes from each of the lessons of the five teachers.

To repeat what I have said earlier, the main aim of VITAL is to give teachers a vehicle for looking at other teachers and as a result reflecting on their own classroom practice. If teachers benefit from this reflection then this in itself is enough and the principal reason why I embarked on the project. It is my strongly held view that we can all benefit from looking at the differing and similar practices we all adopt in the classroom. Observing teachers who adopt similar classroom management approaches to our own can be as rewarding as looking at teachers who employ different methods. It reassures us that our own classroom styles and management techniques are effectively employed by others, and in addition it can allow us to fine-tune these techniques. VITAL has as its strong central basis the detailed work carried out by Hay McBer. By looking at and concentrating on developing the factors the Hay McBer Report highlighted, we can all be confident that we are moving in the right direction.

One way of approaching the extended video highlights is to use the observation form and guidance which I have provided in Appendix 2. The form and guidance are based on the Hay McBer categories of 'Teaching Skills', 'Professional Characteristics' and 'Classroom Climate'. (In the analysis of each teacher that I have provided earlier, I have concentrated on 'Teaching Skills' and 'Professional Characteristics' for the reasons I outlined.) I would suggest that you may benefit from using this form as you look at a particular VITAL teacher and write evidence for the particular 'Teaching Skills', 'Professional Characteristics' and 'Classroom Climate' you observe. You may then wish to refer back to the observations I have made about the particular teacher in this manual. For work in your own school this form could then either be used as it stands or adapted by you or your school as a basis for carrying out 'Self Evaluation' analysis, 'Monitoring and Evaluation' analysis or peer observation analysis of teaching styles in your school. You may then build up a catalogue of the kinds of expertise in particular teaching style areas ('Teaching Skills', 'Professional Characteristics', or 'Classroom Climate') in your school so that all teachers will know where to go to see particular aspects of teacher effectiveness in the school. This sharing of good practice is to me crucial for the development of teaching and learning in schools.

You may on the other hand be about to apply to go through the 'Threshold' as a teacher, and I have attached an example of a blank Threshold Application form together with two examples of ways in which you may like to think about filling in your own form (Appendix 1). You may wish to use the video evidence of teachers in VITAL to think about how you could most effectively move towards this important milestone in your teaching career.

If 'Performance Management' is something you are concerned with (either as an individual wishing to make progress having already gone through the 'Threshold', or as someone with responsibility in your school for managing and assisting teachers with their 'Performance Management') then you could once again use the form and guidance I have provided based on the Hay McBer factors (Appendix 2) or, alternatively, the Performance Management form (Appendix 3). For completeness I have included (Appendix 4) a copy of the OSTED style observation form. This form, which you will see does not have a structure for observation on the form itself, involves observations of teaching, learning, attainment and attitudes and behaviour – though of course you could concentrate on only one aspect. The details of the particular headings to use with this form is given in the 'Lesson Observation Aid'.

To me these are all tools to assist the sharing of good practice in schools and helping us all to become better teachers. You may ultimately wish to use one of these forms and guidance or alternatively you could devise your own system which could be an amalgamation of these.

Appendix 1

Threshold application forms

A   EXAMPLE 1: A blank Threshold application form

B   EXAMPLE 2: A completed Threshold application form

C   EXAMPLE 3: A completed Threshold application form

EXAMPLE 1: BLANK THRESHOLD ASSESSMENT APPLICATION FORM

IMPORTANT: PLEASE READ THE ENCLOSED GUIDANCE NOTES BEFORE STARTING TO COMPLETE THE APPLICATION FORM. This form is also available electronically on the Internet at www.dfee.gov.uk/teachingreforms

THIS APPLICATION FORM SHOULD BE HANDLED IN CONFIDENCE AT ALL TIMES.

Access to this form will be restricted to those who are playing a part in the assessment and verification process.

Personal Details

Surname   First Name(s)

Home Address/Telephone/e:mail/fax

DfEE/Welsh Office Teacher Reference Number

Career Details

Current post

Date joined present school   Length in Post

If not in school, current post and last teaching post (please give dates)

Subject or area specialism, if relevant

Name and Location of School (or other employer)

Name of head

Primary   Secondary   Other

Equal Opportunities Monitoring

The DfEE is committed to equal opportunities. We would like to monitor the profile of those applying for threshold assessment and the outcomes.

To enable us to do this, please complete the enclosed equal opportunities questionnaire and pass it to your headteacher who will forward it with your application form. The information you give us will be treated as confidential and will not form part of the application process.

Data Protection Act 1998

The Department for Education and Employment will process the information collected in this document for the purpose of assessing and monitoring teachers' applications to cross the performance threshold. This information will be processed only within the terms of the Department's Data Protection notification.

1. KNOWLEDGE AND UNDERSTANDING

Please summarise evidence that you:

- **have a thorough and up-to-date knowledge of the teaching of your subject(s) and take account of wider curriculum developments which are relevant to your work.**

Assessment by headteacher, noting any areas for further development.

Standard Met/Not Yet Met

2. TEACHING AND ASSESSMENT

Please summarise evidence

- **plan lessons and sequences of lessons to meet pupils' individual learning needs**

- **use a range of appropriate strategies for teaching and classroom management**

- **use information about prior attainment to set well-grounded expectations for pupils and monitor progress to give clear and constructive feedback.**

(continue on a second page if necessary)

Assessment by headteacher, noting any areas for further development. Each of the three standards above must be met.

3. PUPIL PROGRESS

Please summarise evidence that
relative to their prior attainment, making progress as good or better than similar pupils nationally.   This should be shown in marks or grades in any relevant national tests or examinations, or school based assessment for pupils where national tests and examinations are not taken.

Assessment by headteacher, noting any areas for further development.

Standard Met/Not Yet Met

4. WIDER PROFESSIONAL EFFECTIVENESS

Please summarise evidence that you:

- **take responsibility for your professional development and use the outcomes to improve your teaching and pupils' learning**

- **make an active contribution to the policies and aspirations of your school.**

Assessment by headteacher, noting any areas for further development. Both standards must be met.

Standards Met/Not Yet Met

5. PROFESSIONAL CHARACTERISTICS

Much of what you have said earlier in this form will give information about the professional characteristics you show in your teaching. Please give any further examples here of how you:

challenge and support all pupils to do their best through

inspiring trust and confidence
building team commitment
engaging and motivating pupils
analytical thinking
positive action to improve the quality of pupils' learning.

Assessment by headteacher, taking account of each aspect above and noting any areas for further development.

Standard Met/Not Yet Met

Declaration by applicant

I certify that I am eligible for assessment and that the information in this form is correct. I would like the evidence I have presented to be taken into account in assessing my work against the threshold standards. I understand that further pay progression on the upper pay range will be awarded on the basis of performance and accept that my annual reviews will be used to inform such judgements.

Signed .... Date ....

Declaration by headteacher (or equivalent if not in school)

Applicant name: ……………………………..

School: ……………………………………….

Please explain what evidence additional to this form you have taken into account, e.g. discussion with team leader, appraisal/performance review. Note how the evidence takes account of classroom performance. Set the teacher's performance in the overall context of the achievements of your school. Indicate whether, to the best of your knowledge, the information provided by the applicant is correct, that it derives from the applicant's own practice, and is representative of their overall performance.

Please make a final recommendation in the relevant box below. To be successful applicants must meet each of the standards

Threshold Standards Met   ☐

Not yet Met   ☐

Signed   ………………………………………..   Date …………………………………….

Print name   ……………………………………   School name ………………………….

EXAMPLE 2: A COMPLETED THRESHOLD ASSESSMENT APPLICATION FORM

IMPORTANT: PLEASE READ THE ENCLOSED GUIDANCE NOTES BEFORE STARTING TO COMPLETE THE APPLICATION FORM. This form is also available electronically on the Internet at www.dfee.gov.uk/teachingreforms

THIS APPLICATION FORM SHOULD BE HANDLED IN CONFIDENCE AT ALL TIMES.

Access to this form will be restricted to those who are playing a part in the assessment and verification process.

Personal Details

Surname: First Name(s):

Home Address/Telephone/e:mail/fax:

DfEE/Welsh Office Teacher Reference Number:

Career Details

Current post:

Date joined present school: Length in Post:

If not in school, current post and last teaching post (please give dates)

Subject or area specialism, if relevant:

Name and Location of School (or other employer):
Name of head:

Type of school:

Equal Opportunities Monitoring

The DfEE is committed to equal opportunities. We would like to monitor the profile of those applying for threshold assessment and the outcomes.

To enable us to do this, please complete the enclosed equal opportunities questionnaire and pass it to your headteacher who will forward it with your application form. The information you give us will be treated as confidential and will not form part of the application process.

Data Protection Act 1998

The Department for Education and Employment will process the information collected in this document for the purpose of assessing and monitoring teachers' applications to cross the performance threshold. This information will be processed only within the terms of the Department's Data Protection notification.

1. KNOWLEDGE AND UNDERSTANDING

Please summarise evidence that you:

- **have a thorough and up-to-date knowledge of the teaching of your subject(s) and take account of wider curriculum developments which are relevant to your work.**

A. **I have a sound and up-to-date knowledge of good teaching techniques and how these can be used in my own subject and in teaching in general.**
- I have personally devised a project that I will be working on this coming year in Leeds. *(A copy of the project is available in my portfolio.)*
- I have worked closely with Mr D (from the Raising Achievement Division in Leeds) and will continue to do so this coming year.
- I have, over the past year, visited a number of schools in Leeds to observe effective classroom practitioners.
- I have organised a highly successful training morning (on May 19th 2000) for 15 staff at the school, bringing in Mrs E to introduce the thinking skills developed by Edward de Bono.

B. **I know my subject in sufficient depth to teach effectively.**
- I always incorporate into lessons, examples of how physics is of relevance in the world around us through personal examples if possible. For example, how ultrasound was used to scan my children before they were born (I bring in the photographs I have from these scans), or how radioactive materials have been used to treat cancer.
- I have studied, as part of an MEd at the University of Leeds, how children learn concepts in science. This has made me particularly aware of the concepts which children bring with them to lessons and how these are only to a certain extent modified by the "science" which they are taught. *(My detailed views on this are in my portfolio.)*
- I have helped the HoD in Physics to develop the schemes of work and added worksheets and tests which are used by the whole department.
- I use "Egg Races" (last year with year 7 and previously with year 9) and SATIS to stimulate students. *(Copies of SATIS I have used are in my office.)*
- I successfully and confidently teach students across the whole age range from year 7 to the upper sixth.

C. **I have a broad experience of teaching in a number of secondary schools.**
- 4 years of teaching at C School, 11 years of teaching at F School and 3 years of teaching at G School. This has enabled me to see and study a broad range of effective teaching styles.

D. **I am interested in and aware of national strategies relevant to my teaching and work as a Head of Key Stage 4.**
- Through my work as a governor at my own children's primary school – the literacy and numeracy strategies have had a great impact here and this impact will influence the work we do in secondary schools. I consider that introducing pupils to the specific language of physics and the application of number work in real situations is a key part of my work.
- Through serving on the Academic Board in C School.
- Through serving on the SEN committee.

Assessment by headteacher, noting any areas for further development.

Standard Met/Not Yet Met

2. TEACHING AND ASSESSMENT

Please summarise evidence that you consistently and effectively:

• plan lessons and sequences of lessons to meet pupils' individual learning needs

A. **I use a personally devised "Lesson Planning Sheet" to ensure continuity in my lessons and to target individuals and groups.**
- These incorporate references to the SoWs.
- They also break the structure of the lessons down into activity-segments, which are given time allocations.
- Classroom and homework sheets and other references from texts are given.
- The framework which this gives is flexibly used within the lesson to allow for the development of work and questions which any individual class can bring to the lesson.

(Example of this in my portfolio).

B. **I communicate learning objectives clearly to pupils.**
- I give the pupils a summary of what they are to learn during the course of the lesson at the start of the lesson (I often ask pupils to write this in their books).

(A copy of a page from a typical pupil's book is in my prepared portfolio.)
- At the end of the lesson I summarise what has been learnt myself or ask pupils to do this for the class.

C. **I make effective use of homework and other opportunities for learning outside the classroom.**
- I set exercises where the pupils have to find information out for themselves (including using Encarta and other reference sources).
- I set homeworks which are differentiated and allow students to investigate topics to varying degrees.

(Examples of these homework points in my portfolio).

D. **I have built-up over my teaching career a set of files which incorporate all the work for each section of the GCSE and 'A' level syllabuses**
- These include worksheets and question sheets.
- They also include experimental exercises and additional information from a number of sources.

(These files are readily available for inspection in my office).

• use a range of appropriate strategies for teaching and classroom management

A. **I have a good understanding of the most effective lesson structures, classroom teaching strategies and methods of motivating pupils.**
- I have read a number of recent publications (and watched videos) concerning good teaching practice and new ideas. *(eg. Accelerated Learning in the Classroom by Alistair Smith, Closing the Learning Gap by Mike Hughes, Succeeding with Difficult Pupils by Lee Cantor, training videos by Bill Rogers and Robert Powell.)*
- This coming year I will be carrying out a project in Leeds with the Raising Achievement Division. *(A copy of the project is available in my portfolio)*
- I regularly use mind-map techniques and acrostics in my classroom to encourage learning. I also regularly use pair-work, group-work and brainstorming techniques to complement the traditional format of science lessons. My view is that this enables more pupils of varying abilities and gender to access the concepts in physics. (The Head of Science is aware of these strategies I use.)

B. **I always encourage and support pupils by giving positive feedback at all times whilst dealing with examples of misbehaviour promptly and effectively.**
- Verbally in the classroom I praise, encourage and raise pupils' self-esteem and confidence by the very good rapport I establish with them.
- I boost confidence in classes by encouraging pupils to take a pride in their work.
- I use personally created "stickers" in the books of pupils. (Copies of these "stickers" are available in my portfolio.)
- I create a safe classroom environment where mutual respect is an essential element. In my work as Head of KS4 I also insist on positive behaviour at all times.

C. **I am aware of the semiotics of the classroom environment and its influence on learning and I use this as a positive learning tool.**
- I believe the way a teacher dresses sets a tone and atmosphere and I always dress in a smart and business-like fashion.
- The use of music and a variety of teaching approaches (mentioned above) once again helps me to establish an environment which accommodates the predominant aural, visual or kinaesthetic learning styles of individual pupils. *(The Head of Science is aware of my use of music.)*

2. TEACHING AND ASSESSMENT (CONTINUED)

Please summarise evidence that you **consistently** and **effectively**:

use information about prior attainment to set well-grounded expectations for pupils and monitor progress to give clear and constructive feedback.

A. I always use my knowledge of pupils' individual learning needs to plan lessons and sequences of lessons (and thereby to target individual pupils and groups to ensure good year–on-year progression).
- I change my lesson plans when necessary to accommodate the individual needs and responses of pupils during the course of the lessons.
- I use extension tasks for the most able. *(My worksheets demonstrate this and are available in my office for observation.)*
- The progress and transition of pupils from one year to another is discussed during departmental meetings.
- I analyse the results of the pupils I teach to ensure that they are on or above the targets previously set for them.
- I use the information supplied by the SEN department concerning pupils on the Leeds Matrix together with IEP's to accommodate pupils with individual learning needs in my lesson plans. I keep the Leeds Matrix information in my office and the IEP's of pupils I teach in my teaching file.

B. I report clearly and in detail to parents and pupils concerning attainment and effort.
- I consider and use the school reporting process as a vital tool to inform parents about the progress of their son/daughter in addition to the feedback I provide on an ongoing basis verbally.
- I set and mark homework regularly and I feed back to pupils detailed information in their exercise books based on departmental marking policies, coupled with individual and personal guidance for improvement. *(Copies of homework are in my portfolio.)*

C. As the Head of Key Stage 4 I report to parents concerning the achievement of their son/daughter.
- I send positive letters home to parents when I have analysed the production of interim and final report from teachers, and also when pupils carry out difficult tasks such as reading in assemblies. *(Copies of typical letters are in my portfolio.)*
- The letters following reports are based on the effort (and attainment within their ability range) of pupils rather than just their achievement in subjects.
  (Evidence of the effectiveness of the letters I send home and how well-received they are by parents is available from Mr G, the Deputy Headteacher.)

Assessment by headteacher, noting any areas for further development. Each of the three standards above must be met.

Standard Met/Not Yet Met

3. PUPIL PROGRESS

Please summarise evidence that **as a result of your teaching your pupils achieve well relative to their prior attainment, making progress as good or better than similar pupils nationally. This should be shown in marks or grades in any relevant national tests or examinations, or school based assessment for pupils where national tests and examinations are not taken.**

❖ **Class example 1:** *Year 11 single GCSE science group who took their GCSE in physics in 1999.*
- **Actual progress:** 13 pupils out of 18 had a positive residual from the information provided in the school by Mr H. That is, 13 pupils achieved better in physics than they did on average in other subjects in the school. Using baseline data and comparing the outcomes at GCSE with CAT predictions none of the pupils I taught achieved a grade lower than was predicted.
- **Evaluation of progress:** The group had an overall average substantial positive residual of 0.24. This equates to a total positive residual for the group of 4.56 – that is, the group I taught gained over 4.5 GCSE grades in physics than they did on average in other subjects they took in the school. The CAT data shows that of the 18 pupils in the group 13 achieved a grade in physics above that predicted. In fact the total value-added effect of my teaching was 18 grades improvement for the group above the predicted grades from CATS.

❖ **Class example 2:** *Year 11 dual award GCSE science group who took their GCSE in science in 1999. (This group was taught by myself and two other teachers – in biology and chemistry).*
- **Actual progress:** 13 pupils out of 20 had a positive residual from the information provided in the school by Mr Casey. That is, 13 pupils achieved better in science than they did on average in other subjects in the school. Using baseline data and comparing the outcomes at GCSE with CAT predictions the pupils on the whole achieved grades above those predicted.
- **Evaluation of progress:** The group had an overall positive residual of 0.49. This equates to a total positive residual for the group of 9.8 – that is the group I taught gained over 9.8 GCSE grades in science than they did on average in other subjects they took in the school. Two pupils in this group achieved GCSE grades which were two levels above those predicted from the CATS.

The pupils in both the groups above therefore achieved, on average, better than they did in other subjects in the school and better those grades predicted from CATS. This was the case even though C School pupils achieved extremely well (according to PANDA information provided to the school), above the national average and above the level of comparable schools in 1999.

(Photocopies of the results for both of the classes above, together with the residuals and CAT predictions, are in my portfolio.)

❖ **Class example 3:** *'A' level physics group who took their 'A' level in 1999. (This group was taught by myself and one other teacher).*
- **Actual progress:** 7 students took a physics 'A' level in 1999. Of these, 3 achieved a top A grade, 1 got a B and 2 got a C.
- **Evaluation of progress:** 4 of the students achieved A'level grades which were well above the grades their GCSE points score suggested. Their total value added 'A' level points score was 7.75 (equivalent to nearly 4 A level grades of improvement between the 4 students). The other three students achieved grades only just below their predicted grades from GCSE results.

(Details and analysis of these A'level results is in my portfolio.)

Assessment by headteacher, noting any areas for further development.

Standard Met/Not Yet Met

---

4. WIDER PROFESSIONAL EFFECTIVENESS

Please summarise evidence that you:

- **take responsibility for your professional development and use the outcomes to improve your teaching and pupils' learning**

A. **I view it as important to share examples of good classroom management practice in the school.**
- This coming year I will be the Coordinator of a project in Leeds. This will be supported by Leeds Education Authority and Leeds Metropolitan University. This project has been devised by me and has been developed over the past year.

B. **I believe that it is important to give certain pupils additional support which can make a significant difference to their potential examination outcomes.**
- I am in charge of the mentoring process involving teachers in my school.
- I also coordinate an external-mentoring scheme involving people from industry mentoring year 10 pupils.

C. **I have arranged a number of additional evenings for parents of year 9 and year 7 pupils. This has given me valuable professional development along with other teachers who I asked to take part in the evenings.**
- These took place for the first time last year in the Summer term and the object was to suggest ways for parents to help their son/daughter with homework, as well as allowing parents to get together and discuss certain issues with each other in an informal environment.
- The attendance was very good with over 100 parents coming along on each of the evenings. *(Copies of booklets I produced for these evenings are available in my portfolio and evidence for the success of these evenings can be gained from Mrs C.)*

D. **I am part of a 5-person group (including the Headteacher, a Deputy Headteacher and two senior teachers) which has worked on a bid for Technology College status for the school this coming year.**
- If successful, I would be given the responsibility (along with another Senior Teacher) of overseeing the establishment of further links with the community and the development of the bid through rigorous monitoring and evaluation procedures over the next 4 years.

- **make an active contribution to the policies and aspirations of your school.**

A. **I consider that I make a valuable contribution to the school through my work as the Head of Key Stage 4.**
- By being a representative for the school in my work with parents.
- By setting a set of guidelines for pupils which will influence their behaviour and conduct in school.
- I have contributed to the school discipline policy, home school agreement, anti-bullying statement and anti-racism statement through the Pastoral Management Group.

B. **I believe that in my own teaching it is important to be aware of issues which can influence the learning and development of pupils, and in addition to encourage other teachers to embrace new ideas and good practice.**
- As previously stated, through my work on the Technology College bid.
- As previously stated, through my project in Leeds.
- As previously stated, through my broad reading of issues involving good teaching practice.
- As previously stated, through the additional evenings I have developed for parents at C School.
- As previously stated, through the Edward de Bono training morning I organised.

C. **I use ICT extensively in my work as a Head of Key Stage.**
- A lot of my work concerning the internal exams utilises WORD. *(Evidence available in my office.)*
- I have presented a number of evenings to parents using PowerPoint. ("Options Evening" for parents of year 9 pupils, "Into GCSEs Evening" for parents of pupils about to start their GCSEs, and "Starting Out Evening" for the parents of pupils who have just started at the school.) *(Copies of all of these are available in my portfolio.)*
- I use the Management Information System to Coordinate the options process in year 9.

D. **I believe it is important to emphasise the positive and reward pupils whenever possible.**
- I initiated a system of certificates for pupils in years 10 and 11. Teachers award these to pupils for good work. A record of all certificates received by pupils is kept in the pastoral department and letters of congratulation sent home at key times during the year. Parents have commented very favourably on the system of letters being sent home. *(The Pastoral Deputy Headteacher can verify this and copies of letters sent home are in my portfolio.)*

Assessment by headteacher, noting any areas for further development. Both standards must be met.

Standards Met/Not Yet Met

5. PROFESSIONAL CHARACTERISTICS

Much of what you have said earlier in this form will give information about the professional characteristics you show in your teaching. Please give any further examples here of how you:

challenge and support all pupils to do their best through

inspiring trust and confidence
building team commitment
engaging and motivating pupils
analytical thinking
positive action to improve the quality of pupils' learning.

A. I believe I inspire trust and confidence which enables pupils to work in a secure environment and teachers and parents to have faith in my professional approach.
- I set high standards for pupils in my work as a classroom teacher and as the Head of Key Stage 4.
- I believe that colleagues and pupils view me as an optimistic and positive individual and one who is also approachable, sensitive and supportive.
- I give pupils the freedom and confidence to learn by creating a well structured and caring classroom environment .
- I expect and attain high standards of discipline and behaviour.
- I have always received very positive feedback from parents (e.g. at Parent/Teacher consultation evenings).

B. I build a team commitment with colleagues and pupils.
- One way I do this is through my work as the Head of Key Stage 4 which involves me giving support to the form tutors, classroom teachers and pupils.
- I also do this through my general classroom approach, which emphasises the need for each individual to contribute to the group ethos.

C. I use a variety of opportunities including assemblies to engage and motivate pupils and to set an ethos for pupils built on mutual respect and good manners.
- Teachers and pupils have given me positive feedback following assemblies.
- As a pastoral head, I have worked extremely hard to motivate pupils who are disaffected and often socially excluded.

D. I am constantly aware of the need to use analytical thinking to improve my teaching and the teaching of my colleagues.
- I have a deep interest in looking at the most effective methods of classroom management. *(Reading books mentioned earlier such as "Accelerated Learning", the "VITAL" project I have devised, bringing in a representative of Edward de Bono to talk to teachers in the school and part of my new role in school this next year to disseminate good classroom practice).*

E. My teaching techniques have received favourable feedback over a number of years and from a variety of sources but I am constantly aware of the need to improve the quality of pupils' learning.
- I received a "Distinction" in my early days of teaching during my PGCE teaching practice.
- Recently my OFSTED grades were very positive.
- Feedback from Mrs J, Headteacher, has been encouraging.

Assessment by headteacher, taking account of each aspect above and noting any areas for further development.

Standard Met/Not Yet Met

Declaration by applicant

I certify that I am eligible for assessment and that the information in this form is correct. I would like the evidence I have presented to be taken into account in assessing my work against the threshold standards. I understand that further pay progression on the upper pay range will be awarded on the basis of performance and accept that my annual reviews will be used to inform such judgements.

Signed ………………………………………….   Date …………………………………………

Declaration by headteacher (or equivalent if not in school)

Applicant name: ……………………………..

School: …………………………………………

Please explain what evidence additional to this form you have taken into account, e.g. discussion with team leader, appraisal/performance review. Note how the evidence takes account of classroom performance. Set the teacher's performance in the overall context of the achievements of your school. Indicate whether, to the best of your knowledge, the information provided by the applicant is correct, that it derives from the applicant's own practice, and is representative of their overall performance.

Please make a final recommendation in the relevant box below. To be successful applicants must meet each of the standards

Threshold Standards Met   ☐

Not yet Met   ☐

Signed ……………………………………..   Date ……………………………………….

Print name ………………………………..   School name ……………………………

EXAMPLE 3: A COMPLETED THRESHOLD ASSESSMENT APPLICATION FORM

IMPORTANT: PLEASE READ THE ENCLOSED GUIDANCE NOTES BEFORE STARTING TO COMPLETE THE APPLICATION FORM. This form is also available electronically on the Internet at www.dfee.gov.uk/teachingreforms

THIS APPLICATION FORM SHOULD BE HANDLED IN CONFIDENCE AT ALL TIMES.

Access to this form will be restricted to those who are playing a part in the assessment and verification process.

Personal Details

Surname: First Name(s):

                                        Home Address/Telephone/e:mail/fax:

DfEE/Welsh Office Teacher Reference Number:

Career Details

Current post:

Date joined present school: Length in Post:

If not in school, current post and last teaching post (please give dates)

Subject or area specialism, if relevant:

Name and Location of School (or other employer):

Name of head:

Primary   Secondary   Other

Equal Opportunities Monitoring

The DfEE is committed to equal opportunities. We would like to monitor the profile of those applying for threshold assessment and the outcomes.

To enable us to do this, please complete the enclosed equal opportunities questionnaire and pass it to your headteacher who will forward it with your application form. The information you give us will be treated as confidential and will not form part of the application process.

Data Protection Act 1998

The Department for Education and Employment will process the information collected in this document for the purpose of assessing and monitoring teachers' applications to cross the performance threshold. This information will be processed only within the terms of the Department's Data Protection notification.

1. KNOWLEDGE AND UNDERSTANDING

Please summarise evidence that you:

- have a thorough and up-to-date knowledge of the teaching of your subject(s) and take account of wider curriculum developments which are relevant to your work

I maintain a high level of fluency in French and I constantly update my knowledge of the language and culture, both essential in the teaching of my subject.
- Each year I visit France for a number of weeks and stay with a French family.
- I regularly read French newspapers, magazines and periodicals kept in the departmental files. These keep me up-to-date with topical issues and I use many articles with classes.
- I browse the Internet and download articles to use with the 6th form. e.g. I have recently used an article and statistics concerning the death penalty in France and the USA when discussing capital punishment with Yr. 12 "AS" classes.
- I refer to the departmental library of publications on language teaching methodology *(available in Staff Room)*, and use ideas with my classes to help improve their oral fluency.

I use and have incorporated ICT into my teaching across the whole age range from 11 to 18 in order to improve and consolidate the listening skills and grammatical knowledge of pupils, encourage independent learning and increase motivation.
- I use the Internet to assist 'A' level coursework.
- I have used text manipulation software ("Fun with Texts") with the 2nd (year 8) to 4th year (year 10) this year and with the 1st (year 7) to 4th year (year 10) last year.
- I use CD ROM software ("French Grammar Studio") with years 8 to 13.
- I use the "Virtual Language Laboratory" with years 12 and 13.
- I have used "Pin Point " with year 8 this year.
- I attended a one-day course this year at Salford concerning how to use ICT effectively to raise standards in MFL. I have shared the information with my colleagues and put this into practice in my lessons.
    (Records in the ICT department confirm the above.)

I am aware of the national strategies of literacy and numeracy and have incorporated them into my teaching.
- I encourage students to look at how language functions. With all years, I reinforce semantics and a knowledge of grammatical terms. e.g. Yr. 12 have analysed articles, classing words into grammatical categories *(see portfolio).*
- With all years, I emphasise the importance of spelling and punctuation, *(exercise books/ tests)*, and discuss etymology, false friends etc.
- I encourage personal research using a dictionary, explaining its use, terminology etc.*(worksheets in portfolio).*
- I use many number games and quizzes which consolidate vocabulary and encourage mental agility e.g. Yrs 10-13 play the TV game "Countdown".
- I introduce French money, speak of exchange rates (Yr. 8); students add up bills when acting out scenes at the café, shops etc.

I have kept up to date with curriculum changes including Curriculum 2000 post 16.
- I have participated in discussions concerning the new MFL curriculum.
- I have attended twilight sessions concerning Curriculum 2000
- I have updated the year 7 scheme of work *(available for inspection)* during 1999. The department and I have put this into practice.

Assessment by headteacher, noting any areas for further development.

Standard Met/Not Yet Met

2. TEACHING AND ASSESSMENT

Please summarise evidence that you **consistently** and **effectively**:

- **plan lessons and sequences of lessons to meet pupils' individual learning needs**

My files show that I plan lessons and sequences of lessons effectively to meet the needs of each whole group and the individuals within each group.
- I use extension tasks for the most able and for those pupils with an extensive previous knowledge of French. I have used (during 1998-1999) separate workbooks for year 7 pupils with 2/3 years knowledge. *(Copies in departmental files.)*
- I formulated a separate programme of study for 2 year 11 students preparing for "AS" level who achieved a grade "A". (1998-99).
- I have produced separate worksheets/tests for a year 11 student with dyslexia (1997-98) who achieved a " C" GCSE.
- I have differentiated within my set 4 GCSE group (1999-00), setting different tasks / worksheets / tests to meet the needs of those pupils of lower ability and to raise their self-confidence in the subject.

I communicate learning objectives clearly to pupils.
- I give the pupils a summary of what they are to learn during the course of the lesson/sequence of lessons at the start of the lesson/sequence.
- At the end of the lesson, I give a résumé of what has been achieved or ask pupils to do this for the class. This gives my pupils a clear sense of progression in their learning.

I make effective use of homework and other learning opportunities.
- I regularly set and mark appropriate homework tasks. *(See lesson plans, pupils' books and colleagues' observation sheets)*, to allow pupils to review / consolidate classwork at their own pace.
- I feed back to pupils detailed information in their books based on departmental policy *(SoW and exercise books)*, coupled with individual and personal guidance for improvement.
- I make use of opportunities for learning outside of the classroom by setting personal research for groups - Yr. 13 coursework, Yr. 7 research into various aspects of French life (1999).

- **use a range of appropriate strategies for teaching and classroom management**

I employ a full range of teaching methods to enthuse and motivate pupils.
- I exploit whole class question/answer work, pair-work, group work, ICT the Internet, flashcards, OHP, audio/video resources, drama, quizzes, grammar explanation as tools in the learning process *(see lesson plans, SoW, colleague observation sheets.)*

I have a sound and up-to-date knowledge of good teaching practices and techniques and how to enthuse pupils with a love of French and learning in general and have put these ideas into practice.
- I have read a number of recent publications (and watched videos) concerning good teaching practice and new ideas. *(e.g.Accelerated Learning in the Classroom* by Alistair Smith, *Closing the Learning Gap* by Mike Hughes, *Succeeding with Difficult Pupils* by Lee Cantor, training videos by Bill Rogers.)*
- I refer to the Departmental library (Staff Room) regarding language teaching methodology.
- I have experimented with using music (Yr. 11) and mind-map techniques *(Yrs 9-11)* in my classroom to encourage learning. (I have discussed this with my Head of Department)
- I involve the "assistante" in team lessons (Yrs 8 and 12 during1999/2000), which encourages interest and shows the pupils the true communicative nature of language.

I always encourage and support pupils by giving positive feedback at all times.
- Verbally in the classroom I praise, and raise pupils' self-esteem and confidence by the "very good rapport I establish with them" *(see observation sheets)*.
- I "expect and attain high levels of behaviour and concentration", and I maintain discipline in a quiet, effective way –due to the "obviously very good relationship" that I build with classes *(observation sheets)*.
- I encourage motivation by displaying good examples of pupils' work on the walls in my classroom, which I utilise to the maximum effect with posters and prompts in French
- I use personally created stickers in the books of pupils to encourage motivation and create a sense of pride in their work *(see exercise books)*.

I am aware of the semiotics of the classroom environment and its influence on learning and I use this as a positive learning tool.
- I arrange the seating in such a way that a variety of learning experiences can be easily accessed.
- I utilise my classroom walls to the maximum with bright posters and pupils' work.
- I believe the way a teacher dresses sets a tone and atmosphere and I always dress in a smart and business-like fashion.

2. TEACHING AND ASSESSMENT (continued)

Please summarise evidence

- **use information about prior attainment to set well-grounded expectations for pupils and monitor progress to give clear and constructive feedback.**

I always use my knowledge of pupils' individual learning needs to plan lessons and sequences of lessons.
- Departmental record book, school records, unit test scores (produced for each pupil approximately every 5 weeks), homework and weekly test scores (recorded in my mark book), provide me with a large store of information on which to base my lesson planning and enable me to set targets for pupils.
- I ask pupils to complete individual self-assessment sheets once a year (in files) in which they write targets for improvement and which I monitor.
- I give individual oral assessments to all pupils from Yr. 9-13 *(results in departmental record book)*, which enable me to monitor the progress my pupils have made and target individual needs for future improvement.
- I discuss with colleagues in the department pupils' abilities, progress and attitude as they are transferred so that I can prepare suitable plans and targets, and be aware of group dynamics.

I report clearly and in detail to parents concerning the achievement of their child.
- I use the school reporting process as a vital tool to inform parents about the progress of their child, in addition to the feedback I provide on an ongoing basis verbally and through pupils' exercise books
- I report verbally on student progress to parents on Parent / Teacher consultation evenings.

Assessment by headteacher, noting any areas for further development. Each of the three standards above must be met.

Standard Met/Not Yet Met

3. PUPIL PROGRESS

Please summarise evidence that **as a result of your teaching your pupils achieve well relative to their prior attainment, making progress as good or better than similar pupils nationally. This should be shown in marks or grades in any relevant national tests or examinations, or school based assessment for pupils where national tests and examinations are not taken.**

❖ **Class example 1:** *Year 11 French group (set 4 of 4) who took their GCSE in 1998.*
- **Baseline:** I took the class on at the beginning of Year 11. Their average SAT level at KS3 was 5.9 and the average examination result at the end of Year 10 was 47%
- **Actual progress:** Out of 21 pupils I taught, 18 had a positive residual in French. This means that 18 out of the 21 pupils I taught achieved better grades in the school with me than they did on average in other subjects.
- **Evaluation of progress:** The group had an overall average substantial positive residual of 0.66. The total group residual was +13.81. Again this effectively means that my French class of pupils had a value added effect through my teaching of nearly 14 GCSE grades compared to how they did in other subjects in the school at GCSE. One of the pupils I taught had a positive residual of +2.52 (over 2.5 GCSE grades improvement on what they got in other GCSE examinations) and another + 2.32.

❖ **Class example 2:** *Year 11 French group (set 1 of 4) who took their GCSE in 1999.*
- **Baseline:** I took the class on at the beginning of Year 10. The group had teacher assessed NC levels averaging 6 and SAT levels averaging 7.
- **Actual progress:** All 30 pupils I taught achieved a positive residual. All 30 pupils got a better grade in French than they did on average in other GCSE subjects.
- **Evaluation of progress:** The group had an overall average substantial positive residual of 1.12. This is equivalent to over one grade higher in French at GCSE than in other GCSE subjects. The total group residual was +33.49. . Again this effectively means that my French class of pupils had a value added effect through my teaching of over 33 GCSE grades compared to how they did in other subjects in the school at GCSE. Of the 30 pupils 27 gained an A* and 3 gained an A in French.

According to the PANDA report, the school's overall GCSE results were very high in comparison with schools nationally and with other similar schools in the county. Pupils in both my groups achieved, on average, better in French than in other subjects in the school. Therefore, my classes score well above average and my results are very favourable. County records show that my classes score above those of similar schools in North Yorkshire. *(See HOD.)*

❖ **Class example 3:** *'A' level French group who took their 'A' level in 1999. (This group was taught by myself and one other teacher).*
- Baseline: I took the group from the beginning of Year 12. Out of 11 pupils, 2 had an average GCSE score of 7.2 or more; 5 averaged 6.5-7.1; 4 averaged 6-6.4.
- Actual progress: Of the 11 students taught, 3 achieved a top A grade, 4 got a B, 2 got a C and 2 got a D.
- Evaluation of progress: 7 of the students achieved 'A' level grades which were above the grades their GCSE points score suggested. Their total value added 'A' level points score was 9 (equivalent to 4.5 'A' level grades of improvement between the 7 students). 2 of the students achieved 'A' level grades in complete agreement with what was predicted at GCSE. The other 2 students were just below the 'A' level grades predicted from GCSE. From the whole group I had a net value added figure of 5.75. Again this is equivalent to a total of nearly three 'A' level grades for the whole group.

❖ **Class example 4:** *Year 9 French group 1998-99 (set 3 of 4).*
- Baseline: A group of 27 students who, at the end of Yr. 8, were all working at teacher assessed levels of 4 or 5.
- Actual progress: All students achieved TA level 5 at the end of the year and the set average was 60%
- Evaluation of progress: All pupils achieved the level targeted by departmental policy and the average class percentage was well in line with that of the other Year 9 sets.

(Analysis of all the statistics above is available in my portfolio.)

Assessment by headteacher, noting any areas for further development.

Standard Met/Not Yet Met

4. WIDER PROFESSIONAL EFFECTIVENESS

Please summarise evidence that you:

- **take responsibility for your professional development and use the outcomes to improve your teaching and pupils' learning**

I take a pro-active approach to my own learning and effectiveness as a classroom teacher.
- I maintain and improve my fluency by my annual visit to France - the best source of development for an MFL teacher. This enables me to provide a stimulating, target language environment for my pupils; it gives myself and them up-to-date knowledge of the language and culture and increases proficiency, understanding and interest.
- I accompany visits to MFL "A" level conferences *(Updates 1998/99)* which support the syllabus, widen my knowledge and that of my students.
- I am developing my ICT skill, which is an area where I am largely self-taught. I attended a 1 day course *(see section 1)* and records in the ICT department show that I regularly put my knowledge into use to help reinforce grammar, improve listening skills etc *(see section 1)*.

I am committed to my personal and professional development in education.
- During 1998/99, I shadowed colleagues in the Lower School, enabling me to be aware of the impact of the KS2 curriculum on the work carried out at KS3 and beyond, and to help pupils in the transition progress from primary school.
- In !999, I was successful in my application for the position of Deputy Head of Upper School and Work Experience Co-ordinator. My closer involvement with pupils and parents on a pastoral level has made me more aware of each pupil as an individual, and of the issues outside of school which can affect the learning of pupils in the classroom.
- I attended a 1-day course (1/2/00) concerning "Supporting Students with Eating Disorders" and a course (3/11/99) relating to "Drug and Alcohol Awareness". These have heightened my own awareness of problems which may affect students, and have enabled me to deal more effectively with these problems when they have arisen, and to support the students involved.
- I attended a Health and Safety Awareness day (24/4/99), and am qualified to make KS4 work experience placement visits- an important aspect of my new role as Work Experience Co-ordinator.
- I contributed to the criteria agreed upon for pupils in Yr. 11 to be mentored, and have been a mentor for 2 years. I believe this additional support has made significant differences to the students' potential examination outcomes.

- **make an active contribution to the policies and aspirations of your school.**

I consider that I make a valuable contribution to the school through my work as Deputy Head of Upper School.
- I am a representative for the school in my work with parents, with the ESWO and other outside agencies.
- I contribute to the ethos of the school by implementing a set of guidelines for pupils which will influence their behaviour and conduct in school, whilst lending support and advice where appropriate *(as the Head of Upper School and colleagues will confirm)*. I encourage care and consideration for others and a pride in their own appearance.

I implement school policy and make a valuable contribution by co-ordinating the Work Experience programme.
- I ensure that all pupils receive a suitable placement from which they gain immense value and develop many key skills and interests.
- I represent the school in my dealings with the local community, industry and commerce.
- I organised an information evening for parents dealing with the aims and the process of the Work Experience programme.

I contributed to the departmental observation scheme.
- I was observed on 4 occasions and went into the classrooms of 4 colleagues. This enabled me to witness and to share examples of good classroom practice and participate in raising standards in support of school policy.

I am supportive of all aspects of school life.
- I have always been actively involved in Charity Week activities.
- I have helped at school drama productions (make-up, refreshments etc.).
- I have accompanied the French exchange group on their journey from France.

Assessment by headteacher, noting any areas for further development. Both standards must be met.

Standards Met/Not Yet Met

5. PROFESSIONAL CHARACTERISTICS

Much of what you have said earlier in this form will give information about the professional characteristics you show in your teaching. Please give any further examples here of how you:

challenge and support all pupils to do their best through
    inspiring trust and confidence
    building team commitment
    engaging and motivating pupils
    analytical thinking
    positive action to improve the quality of pupils' learning.

I believe I inspire trust and confidence, which enables pupils to work in a secure environment, and teachers and parents to have faith in my professional approach.
- I set high standards for pupils in my work as a classroom teacher, as Deputy Head of Upper School and W.E. co-ordinator.
- Colleagues and pupils view me as an optimistic, cheerful and positive person and one who is also approachable, sensitive and supportive.
- I give pupils the freedom and confidence to learn by creating a well-structured and caring classroom environment, where there is a "co-operative, pleasant atmosphere" (colleagues' observation).
- I expect and attain high standards of discipline and behaviour. Colleagues have observed that the "good behaviour and concentration come from the obviously excellent rapport built up."
- Feedback from parents (Parent/teacher consultation evenings), pupils and colleagues (observation) has always been positive.

I build a team commitment with colleagues and pupils.
- I do this through my work as Deputy Head of Upper School and W.E. co-ordinator where I work closely with and am supportive of the Head of Upper School, form tutors, classroom teachers and pupils.
- I also do this through my general classroom approach, where I emphasise the need for each individual to contribute to the group ethos, and through my work with my HoD and fellow language teachers. I view it as important and vital to share examples of good practice/new ideas with them and we form a united and happy team.

I use a variety of techniques and approaches to stimulate interest and to motivate the full range of abilities.
- I relate learning to everyday experience e.g. comparing the lives of young French people with my pupils' lives.
- I give opportunities to use song, drama, games, quizzes, audio/video, personal presentation etc. (see section 1). e.g. Yr. 9 have presented TV weather forecasts which I videoed, Yr. 8 invented playlets about French family life.
- I introduced a system of reward certificates, which the department and I use to motivate.

I am aware of the need to use analytical thinking to improve my teaching.
- I have a deep interest in looking at the most effective methods of classroom management (e.g. see books in section 1). I have targeted the underachievement of boys in my Yr. 8 class. I re-arranged the seating, set them short-term learning targets, and used positive reinforcement and praise. Test results, homework, concentration in class demonstrate some improvement in learning.
- I organise lessons where possible into "bite-size" pieces, changing activity every 10-15 minutes to improve concentration.
- At the end of each unit, I review my lessons, note the more/less successful aspects, and use these notes to improve planning.

I am constantly looking for ways to improve my effectiveness and thus the pupils' learning.
- I am increasing my own capabilities in my use of ICT in order to use it as another effective learning tool and to stimulate interest.
- I provide more opportunities for pupils to work as independent learners (readers in Yrs 7-9, CD-ROMs, personal research).

Assessment by headteacher, taking account of each aspect above and noting any areas for further development.

Standard Met/Not Yet Met

Declaration by applicant

I certify that I am eligible for assessment and that the information in this form is correct. I would like the evidence I have presented to be taken into account in assessing my work against the threshold standards. I understand that further pay progression on the upper pay range will be awarded on the basis of performance and accept that my annual reviews will be used to inform such judgements.

Signed ....   Date ....

Declaration by headteacher (or equivalent if not in school)

Applicant name: ……………………………..

School: ……………………………………….

Please explain what evidence additional to this form you have taken into account, e.g. discussion with team leader, appraisal/performance review. Note how the evidence takes account of classroom performance. Set the teacher's performance in the overall context of the achievements of your school. Indicate whether, to the best of your knowledge, the information provided by the applicant is correct, that it derives from the applicant's own practice, and is representative of their overall performance.

Please make a final recommendation in the relevant box below. To be successful applicants must meet each of the standards

Threshold Standards Met ☐

Not yet Met ☐

Signed …………………………………….. Date ……………………………………..

Print name …………………………………. School name …………………………….

Suggested Observation Forms Using the Hay McBer analysis and observation guidance criteria

Date:	Teacher:
Lesson:	Observer:

HAY MCBER - TEACHING SKILLS OBSERVATION FORM	
Heading	**Observations**
1 High expectations	
2 Planning	
3 Methods and strategies	
4 Pupil management/discipline	
5 Time and resource management	
6 Assessment	
7 Homework	

Date:	Teacher:
Lesson:	Observer:

HAY MCBER – PROFESSIONAL CHARACTERISTICS OBSERVATION FORM

	Cluster	Tick Characteristics to be Observed	Observations
1	Professionalism	☐ Challenge and support ☐ Confidence ☐ Creating trust ☐ Respect for others	
2	Thinking	☐ Analytical thinking ☐ Conceptual thinking	
3	Planning and setting expectations	☐ Drive for improvement ☐ Information seeking ☐ Initiative	
4	Leading	☐ Flexibility ☐ Holding people accountable ☐ Managing pupils ☐ Passion for learning	
5	Relating to others	☐ Impact and influence ☐ Teamworking ☐ Understanding others	

Effective Teachers

Date:	Teacher:
Lesson:	Observer:

HAY MCBER – CLASSROOM CLIMATE OBSERVATION FORM

Climate dimension	Observations
1 Clarity	
2 Order	
3 Standards	
4 Fairness	
5 Participation	
6 Support	
7 Safety	
8 Interest	
9 Environment	

Hay McBer Style
Lesson Observation Guidance (Criteria)

HAY MCBER - TEACHING SKILLS – GUIDANCE

	Heading	Key Questions as Guidance

1	High expectations	1. Does the teacher encourage high standards of:
		  - Effort?
		  - Accuracy?
		  - Presentation?
		2. Does the teacher use differentiation appropriately to challenge all pupils in the class?
		3. Does the teacher vary motivational strategies for different individuals?
		4. Does the teacher provide opportunities for students to take responsibility for their own learning?
		5. Does the teacher draw on pupil experiences or ideas relevant to the lesson?

2	Planning	1. Does the teacher communicate a clear plan and objectives for the lesson at the start of the lesson? 2. Does the teacher have the necessary materials and resources ready for the class? 3. Does the teacher link lesson objectives to the national curriculum?
3	Methods and strategies	1. Does the teacher involve all pupils in the lesson? 2. Does the teacher use a variety of activities/ learning methods? 3. Does the teacher apply teaching methods appropriate to the National Curriculum? 4. Does the teacher use a variety of questioning techniques to probe pupils' knowledge and understanding? 5. Does the teacher encourage pupils to use a variety of problem- solving techniques? 6. Does the teacher give clear instructions and explanations? 7. Does practical activity have a clear purpose in improving pupils' understanding or achievement? 8. Does the teacher listen and respond to pupils?
4	Pupil management/ discipline	1. Does the teacher keep pupils on task throughout the lesson? 2. Does the teacher correct bad behaviour immediately? 3. Does the teacher praise good achievement and effort? 4. Does the teacher treat different children fairly? 5. Does the teacher manage non-pupils (support teachers/ staff) well?
5	Time and resource management	1. Does the teacher structure the lesson to use the time available well? 2. Does the lesson last for the planned time? 3. Are the appropriate learning resources used to enhance pupils' opportunities? 4. Does the teacher use an appropriate pace? 5. Does the teacher allocate his/ her time fairly amongst pupils?

6	Assessment	1. Does the teacher focus on:
		  ● understanding and meaning?
		  ● factual memory?
		  ● skills mastery?
		  ● applications in real life settings?
		2. Does the teacher use tests, competitions, etc. to assess understanding?
		3. Does the teacher recognise misconceptions and clear them up?
		4. Is there evidence of pupils' written work having been marked or otherwise assessed?
		5. Does the teacher encourage pupils to do better next time?

7	Homework	1. Is the homework set either to consolidate or extend the coverage of the lesson? 2. Is homework which had been set previously followed up in the lesson? 3. Does the teacher explain what learning objectives pupils will gain from homework?

HAY MCBER – PROFESSIONAL CHARACTERISTICS - GUIDANCE

	Cluster	Tick Characteristics to be Observed	Guidance
1	Professionalism	❑ Challenge and support	A commitment to do everything possible for each pupil and enable all pupils to be successful.
		❑ Confidence	The belief in one's ability to be effective and to take on challenges.
		❑ Creating trust	Being consistent and fair. Keeping one's word.
		❑ Respect for others	The underlying belief that individuals matter and deserve respect.
2	Thinking	❑ Analytical thinking	The ability to think logically, break things down, and recognise cause and effect.
		❑ Conceptual thinking	The ability to see patterns and links, even when there is a lot of detail.
3	Planning and setting expectations	❑ Drive for improvement	Relentless energy for setting and meeting challenging target, for pupils and the school.
		❑ Information seeking	A drive to find out more and get to the heart of things intellectual curiosity.
		❑ Initiative	The drive to act now to anticipate and pre-emt events.
4	Leading	❑ Flexibility	The ability and willingness to adapt to the needs of a situation and change tactics.
		❑ Holding people accountable	The drive and ability to set clear expectations and parameters and to hold others accountable for performance.
		❑ Managing pupils	The drive and the ability to provide clear direction to pupils, and to enthuse and motivate them.
		❑ Passion for learning	The drive and an ability to support pupils in their learning, and how to help become confident and independent learners.
5	Relating to others	❑ Impact and influence	The ability and the drive to produce positive outcomes by impressing and influencing others.
		❑ Teamworking	The ability to work with others to achieve shared goals.
		❑ Understanding others	The drive and ability to understand others, and why they behave as they do.

HAY MCBER – CLASSROOM CLIMATE - GUIDANCE

	Climate dimension	Guidance
1	Clarity	Clarity around the purpose of each lesson. How each lesson relates to the broader subject, as well as clarity regarding the aims and objectives of the school
2	Order	Order within the classroom, where discipline , order and civilised behaviour are maintained.
3	Standards	A clear set of standards as to how pupils should behave and what each pupil should do and try to achieve, with a clear focus on higher rather than minimum standards.
4	Fairness	Fairness: the degree to which there is an absence of favouritism, and a consistent link between rewards in the classroom and actual performance.
5	Participation	Participation: the opportunity for pupils to participate actively in the class by discussion, questioning, giving out materials, and other similar activities.
6	Support	Support: feeling emotionally supported in the classroom, so that pupils are willing to try new things and learn from mistakes.
7	Safety	Safety: the degree to which the classroom is a safe place, where pupils are not at risk from emotional bullying, or other fear- rousing factors.
8	Interest	Interest: the feeling that the classroom is an interesting and exciting place to be, where pupils feel stimulated to learn.
9	Environment	Environment: the feeling that the classroom is a comfortable, well organised, clean and attractive physical environment.

Performance Management Style Lesson Observation Assessment Form

Date:	Teacher:
Lesson:	Observer:

	Excellent	Good	Satisfactory	Development needed	N/A
1 The teacher plans effectively and sets clear objectives					
2 The teacher shows good subject knowledge and understanding					
3 The teaching methods used enable all pupils to learn effectively					
4 Pupils are managed well and high standards of behaviour are insisted on.					
5 Pupils' work is assessed thoroughly.					
6 Pupils achieve productive outcomes.					
7 The teacher makes effective use of time and resources.					
8 Homework is used effectively to reinforce and extend learning.					

Conclusions and Feedback

Strengths:

Areas for Development:

Teacher's comment (optional):

Performance Management Style Lesson Observation Guidance (Criteria)

			Tick Areas to be Observed
1		**The teacher plans effectively and sets clear objectives that are understood.**	
	a	Objectives are communicated clearly at the start of the lesson.	
	b	Materials are ready.	
	c	There is a good structure to the lesson.	
	d	The lesson is reviewed at the end.	
	e	The learning needs of those with Individual Education Plans (EPs) are incorporated in the teacher's planning.	
2		**The teacher shows good subject knowledge and understanding.**	
	a	Teacher has a thorough knowledge of the subject content covered in the lesson.	
	b	Subject material is appropriate for the lesson.	
	c	Knowledge is made relevant and interesting for pupils.	
3		**The teaching methods used enable all pupils to learn effectively.**	
	a	The lesson is linked to previous teaching or learning.	
	b	The ideas and experiences of pupils are drawn upon.	
	c	A variety of activities and questioning techniques is used.	
	d	Instructions and explanations are clear and specific.	
	e	The teacher involves all pupils, listens to them, and responds appropriately.	
	f	High standards of effort, accuracy and presentation are encouraged.	
	g	Appropriate methods of differentiation are used.	
4		**Pupils are managed well and high standards of behaviour are insisted upon.**	
	a	Pupils are praised regularly for their good effort and achievement.	
	b	Prompt action is taken to address poor behaviour.	
	c	All pupils are treated fairly, with equal emphasis on the work of boys and girls, and all ability groups.	
5		**Pupils' work is assessed thoroughly.**	
	a	Teacher uses questions to assess pupils' understanding throughout the lesson.	
	b	Mistakes and misconceptions are recognised by the teacher and used constructively to facilitate learning.	
	c	Pupils' written work is assessed regularly and accurately.	
6		**Pupils achieve productive outcomes.**	
	a	Pupils remain fully engaged throughout the lesson and make progress in the lesson.	
	b	Pupils understand what work is expected of them during the lesson.	
	c	The pupil outcomes from the lesson are consistent with the objectives set at the beginning.	

7	**The teacher makes effective use of time and resources.**	
a	Time is well utilised and the learning is maintained for the full time available.	
b	A good pace is maintained throughout the lesson.	
c	Good use is made of any support available, for example learning assistants and older pupils.	
d	Appropriate learning resources are used, for example, ICT.	
8	**Homework is used effectively to reinforce and extend learning.**	
a	Homework is set, if appropriate.	
b	The learning objectives are explicit and relate to the work in progress.	
c	Homework is followed up if it has been set.	

In addition to Performance Management all these areas will be relevant to Threshold Assessment and in particular:

Threshold Assessment Sections		Relevant Performance Management Areas Above
1	KNOWLEDGE AND UNDERSTANDING	2
2	TEACHING AND ASSESSMENT	1, 3, 4, 5, 7 & 8
3	PUPIL PROGRESS	6
4 & 5	PROFESSIONAL CHARACTERISTICS	1, 3, 4 & 5

OFSTED Style Observation Form and lesson observation aid

Evidence Form					

Inpector's OIN		School URN		Observation Type	L A D O
Year Group(s)		Grouping	A M G S B O	Present/NOR	
Object Codes		Accreditation	GC AL AS VA VI VF VP VO XO	Observation Time	
Teacher's Status	QUTSN	Lesson Type	CL GR IN MI XO	Support Teacher/Staff	
Teacher's Code		Insp's EF No		SIS Input Ref No	

Context

Evidence

When recording grades, use 0 to 7 to reflect judgements in the text on: Teaching; Learning; Attainment; Attitudes and Behaviour

Teaching		Learning		Attainment		Attitudes and Behaviour	

OFSTED Style
Lesson Observation Aid

Context
Briefly describe the lesson and what pupils are doing.

Evidence
Record the evidence you have collected and your judgements made on the basis of that evidence.

Use evaluative words carefully to distinguish, for example, between very good and good, so that someone else would arrive at the same grade and evaluation.

1=excellent; 2=very good; 3=good; 4=satisfactory; 5=unsatisfactory; 6=poor; 7=very poor; 0=no evidence. Synonyms allow for varied, more interesting writing, for example excellent = outstanding, superb; satisfactory = competent, acceptable and so forth.

Focus on strengths and weaknesses of the lesson and indicate what makes them strengths or weaknesses.

Give illustrations, which you can draw on for examples of strengths and weaknesses when giving feedback on the lesson.

Give clear judgements, in accordance with the criteria in the OFSTED Handbook, especially on teaching, learning, attainments, attitudes and behaviour. Write in notes or in continuous prose.

Use all relevant criteria for which you have evidence.

Teaching – consider the extent to which teachers:	Tick Areas to be Observed
• Show good subject knowledge and understanding in presenting and discussing their subject;	
• Are technically competent in teaching basis skills;	
• Plan effectively, setting clear objectives;	
• Challenge and inspire pupils, expecting the most of them so as to deepen their knowledge and understanding	
• Use methods which allow all pupils to learn effectively;	
• Manage pupils well and insist on high standards of behaviour;	
• Use time, support staff and resources, especially ICT, effectively;	
• Assess pupils' work thoroughly and use assessments to help and encourage pupils to overcome difficulties; and	
• Use homework effectively to reinforce and/or extend what is learned in school.	
Learning – consider the extent to which pupils and students:	
• Acquire new knowledge or skills, develop ideas and increase their understanding;	
• Apply intellectual, physical or creative effort in their work;	
• Are productive and work at a good pace;	
• Show interest in their work, are able to sustain concentration and think and learn for themselves; and	
• Understand what they are doing, how well they have done and how they can improve.	

Attainment – consider the extent to which:	
• Results match or exceed the average for all schools;	
• The class is on course to meet challenging targets;	
• Pupils with SEN and with EAL, the gifted and talented make good progress;	
• There are no weaknesses by gender or ethnicity;	
• Results are high in comparison with similar schools, or show significant added value in comparison with earlier results; and	
• Achievements meet or exceed levels set by the National Curriculum the local agreed syllabus for religious education or any examination or assessment objectives.	

Attitudes and behaviour – consider the extent to which pupils and students:	
• Are keen and eager to attend;	
• Show interest and are involved;	
• Behave well, are courteous, trustworthy, and respect property;	
• Form constructive relationships with each other and with teachers;	
• Work in an atmosphere free from oppressive behaviour, bullying, sexism, and racism;	
• Reflect on and understand the impact of what they do on others;	
• Respect other people's differences, particularly their feelings, values and beliefs; and	
• Show initiative and are willing to take responsibility.	

When recording grades, use 0 to 7 to reflect judgements in the text on:

Teaching; Learning; Attainment; Attitudes and Behaviour.

Teaching		Learning		Attainment		Attitudes and behaviour	

Bibliography

Attwood, Tony (1988) *Raising Grades at GCSE*. Northants.: First and Best Publications.

Hughes, Mike (1999) *Closing the Learning Gap*. Stafford: Network Educational Press.

Robbins, Anthony (1986) *Unlimited Power*. London: Simon and Schuster.

Watkins, Chris (2000) *Managing Classroom Behaviour – From Research To Diagnosis*. London: Institute of Education with the Association of Teachers and Lecturers.

Covey, Stephen R. (1989) *The Seven Habits of Highly Effective People*. London: Simon and Schuster.

HH Dalai Lama & Howard Cutler (1998) *The Art of Happiness*. London: Coronet.

Powell, Robert (1997) *Raising Achievement and Active Whole Class Teaching*. Stafford: Robert Powell Publications.

Goleman, Daniel (1996) *Emotional Intelligence*. London: Bloomsbury Publishing.

DfEE Teaching Training Agency (1998) *National Standards for Headteachers*. HMSO.

DfEE (2000) *A Model of Teacher Effectiveness. Report by Hay McBer to the Department for Education and Employment, June 2000*. HMSO.

Other Titles from Network Educational Press

THE SCHOOL EFFECTIVENESS SERIES - Series Editor: **Tim Brighouse**
Book 1: *Accelerated Learning in the Classroom* by Alistair Smith
Book 2: *Effective Learning Activities* by Chris Dickinson
Book 3: *Effective Heads of Department* by Phil Jones & Nick Sparks
Book 4: *Lessons are for Learning* by Mike Hughes
Book 5: *Effective Learning in Science* by Paul Denley and Keith Bishop
Book 6: *Raising Boys' Achievement* by Jon Pickering
Book 7: *Effective Provision for Able & Talented Children* by Barry Teare
Book 8: *Effective Careers Education & Guidance* by Andrew Edwards and Anthony Barnes
Book 9: *Best behaviour and Best behaviour FIRST AID* by
   Peter Relf, Rod Hirst, Jan Richardson and Georgina Youdell
   Best behaviour FIRST AID (pack of 5 booklets)
Book 10: *The Effective School Governor* by David Marriott
   (including free audio tape)
Book 11: *Improving Personal Effectiveness for Managers in Schools* by James Johnson
Book 12: *Making Pupil Data Powerful* by Maggie Pringle and Tony Cobb
Book 13: *Closing the Learning Gap* by Mike Hughes
Book 14: *Getting Started* by Henry Leibling
Book 15: *Leading the Learning School* by Colin Weatherley
Book 16: *Adventures in Learning* by Mike Tilling
Book 18: *Classroom Management* by Philip Waterhouse and Chris Dickinson

ACCELERATED LEARNING SERIES - General Editor: **Alistair Smith**
Accelerated Learning in Practice by Alistair Smith
The ALPS Approach: Accelerated Learning in Primary Schools by Alistair Smith and Nicola Call
MapWise by Oliver Caviglioli and Ian Harris
The ALPS Resource Book by Alistair Smith and Nicola Call
Reaching out to all Learners by Cheshire LEA
Thinking Skills and Eye Cue by Oliver Caviglioli, Ian Harris and Bill Tindall

VISIONS OF EDUCATION SERIES
The Unfinished Revolution by John Abbott and Terry Ryan
The Child is Father of the Man by John Abbott
The Learning Revolution by Jeanette Vos and Gordon Dryden
Wise-Up by Guy Claxton
Power Up Your Mind by Bill Lucas
Schools That Learn by Peter Senge
The Power of Diversity by Barbara Prashing

THE LITERACY COLLECTION
Helping With Reading by Anne Butterworth and Angela White
Class Talk by Rosemary Sage

OTHER TITLES FROM NEP
Effective Resources for Able and Talented Children by Barry Teare
More Effective Resources for Able and Talented Children by Barry Teare
Imagine That... by Stephen Bowkett
Self-Intelligence by Stephen Bowkett
Brain Friendly Revision by UFA National Team